JOHN WESLEY
and his world

JOHN PUDNEY

JOHN WESLEY
and his world

with 125 illustrations

CHARLES SCRIBNER'S SONS
NEW YORK

Printed in Great Britain
Library of Congress Catalog Card Number 78-59110
ISBN 0-684-15922-8

ON AN OCTOBER NIGHT IN 1736, four years after George II had given his name and granted a charter to the American colony of Georgia, a thirty-three-year-old Anglican clergyman, a Fellow of Lincoln College, Oxford, lay in the open on St Katherine's Island in that colony, contemplating a girl of eighteen. His wakefulness was not due to the cold. There was a camp fire, and for all his neat black attire and the elegant slightness of his figure, he was indifferent to discomfort. He was dedicated to God. He and his brother had endured the Atlantic voyage of three and a half months, practising self-denial and preaching to the motley payload of settlers. His duty was to spread the word of God.

The girl Sophy Hopkey was awake too. Across the sleeping bodies of a servant and the crew of the barge-like boat, stranded together on this uninhabited island, she gazed at this enigmatic man of God, the Reverend John Wesley, whom she now found herself so precariously in love with.

At last John Wesley broke the silence:

'Miss Sophy,' he said, 'how far are you engaged to Mr Mellichamp?'

She answered hesitantly: 'I have promised either to marry him or to marry no one at all.'

'Miss Sophy, I should think myself happy if I was to spend my life with you.' Thus he came to the brink of a declaration.

It was not seemly for a young girl to venture beyond delicate negatives. She wept. 'I am every way unhappy,' she sobbed. 'I won't have Tommy, for he is a bad man. And I can have none else. . . .'

But John Wesley did not press the matter. There was some further inconclusive conversation, and then they sang a psalm. Anyone witnessing the bizarre incident in that remote place could never have foreseen that the vacillating young man with the beautiful voice would one day assert: 'I look upon all the world as my parish,' and that on his death the Methodism he founded would have achieved a mighty following both in Great Britain and in America.

At the time of his unsuccessful dalliance with Sophy Hopkey, and his nearly disastrous spell of duty in Georgia, to which we shall return later, there was no indication that he would be one of the outstanding figures of the eighteenth century. The story is well documented. Wesley was a prolific letter-writer and indefatigable in keeping a journal in which he wrote of success and failure, of hope and despair, with a forthrightness which matched his public speaking and was rare at that time in men of his education.

Meanwhile, the affair with Miss Sophy was early evidence that there was scarcely room in his life for a mate, though he attracted women and enjoyed their company. Dominating all his conceptions of womanhood was his mother Susanna. Though she died shortly after the start of his forty years of itinerant preaching across the length and breadth of the British Isles, her influence remained with him throughout his life. Yet her strong character never coerced him to cling to her petticoats. When he and his brother Charles had set out for America she declared: 'If I had twenty sons, I should rejoice that they were all so employed, though I should never see them again.' This was no idle boast, for in that century many who set out for America were never seen again by those in the home country.

As for her reference to 'twenty sons', Susanna Wesley in reality fell only slightly short of her rhetorical declaration. In the course of twenty years of marriage she had nineteen children, of whom only nine survived infancy. John Benjamin Wesley, born 17 (O.S.) June 1703, was the fifteenth child, his brother Charles, born in 1707, the last but one. Susanna was the beautiful and intelligent daughter of Dr Samuel Annesley, a Church of England minister who became a renowned Nonconformist. Large families were no novelty to her, for she was herself the youngest of a brood of twenty-four or twenty-five – even her distinguished Puritan father seemed uncertain of the figure. Answering an enquiry at the time of Susanna's baptism, he said: 'Two dozen, I believe, or a quarter of a hundred.'

Susanna had theology in her blood, and also received an exceptional education. At the early age of thirteen she decided to join the Church of England, but this meant no relaxation of Puritanical austerities. She resolved to spend more time on prayer than on pleasure. Her marriage to Samuel Wesley, a strict Anglican curate who much fancied himself as a poet, enabled her to escape the religious controversy within the family for what must have seemed a freer life. In fact it turned out to be a singularly hard one, taxing all her spiritual and physical resources.

Samuel Wesley was not a bad husband, and he was certainly not a bad man. But he suffered from violent delusions, an uneasy temper, improvidence in worldly things, and an aggressively rigorous attitude to Anglicanism. Having begun his career as a curate in London, he was appointed after a short period to South Ormsby, a hamlet in

Opposite, Susanna Wesley (1669–1742), mother of John, Charles, and seventeen other children. Formidable and gifted, her influence on them all was to be profound.

7

Right, Wesley's father Samuel, inflexible Anglican clergyman and disappointed poet, dedicated a long work on the life of Christ to Queen Mary of Orange (*below*), for which he received the dubious reward of the lifelong tenure of the parish of Epworth (*opposite, below*), a remote and barbarous Fenland village. *Opposite, above,* the frontispiece for his first work, depicting the poet with laurel wreath and gnawing maggot on the brain.

Lincolnshire. But Mr Wesley was also full of poetry. At the age of twenty-two he had published a volume entitled *Maggots.* He went on to compose a heroic poem on the life of Christ, which he dedicated to Queen Mary of Orange. Mr Wesley was duly rewarded with the living of Epworth, and a stipend of £200 a year. But even with the agricultural holding that went with it, this was never enough.

Epworth lies in Lincolnshire, to the south of the Isle of Axholme, a tract of land bounded by rivers, much of it at that time still undrained. It pleased the rector to designate himself the Poet of the Isle of Axholme, or the Island Poet. He was for ever hoping that, dedicated to the right people, his verses might bring him preferment, and this delusion persisted throughout his thirty-nine years as rector of Epworth. This pursuit would have been harmless enough had it brought him either peace of mind or financial reward. But even his rhyming history of the Bible in three duodecimo volumes, dedicated to Queen Anne, failed to advance him as priest or poet. Nor did his flights of imagination ameliorate the severity of his High Church Anglicanism, which he applied to his parishioners with relentless rigour.

Mr Wesley and Susanna shared one painful spiritual ordeal: they had both been brought up as Dissenters and had gone over to the Church of England in defiance of their families. In spite of this a rift between them grew, though never openly, with the years, and Susanna once exclaimed: 'It is a misfortune peculiar to our family that he and I seldom think alike.'

His own background of Dissent made the rector of Epworth particularly aggressive towards the many Dissenters in his parish. They were fen people, rough, uncouth, sullenly aggressive. In the eighteenth century there was little civilization or enlightenment among such isolated communities. The churchgoers among them resented the discipline he tried to impose, which included doing penance by standing barefoot in the aisle of the church. Parishioners jeered at the refinement and culture existing in the poverty-stricken rectory. The parson's debts and his mismanagement of the glebe land aroused

In's own defence the Author writes
Because while this foul Maggot bites
He nere Can rest in quiet,
Which makes him make soe sad a face
He'd beg your worship or your Grace
Unseen to buy it.

Epworth market place. Open
hostility continued for years between
the Rev. Samuel Wesley and his
parishioners.

derision. Nor was that all. Furtive attacks were made. The parson's
cattle were maimed, his field of flax fired. His children were jeered at:
'We'll soon have you out a'begging.'

The rector was not cowed by the hostility he aroused, and lost no
opportunity of flaying his parishioners with his tongue. Within the
family, he was in the habit of offering up a daily prayer for King
William III of Orange. Suddenly in 1701 he noticed that Susanna –
Sukey as he called her – omitted to say Amen. He realized then that
her political opinions and loyalties were resolutely opposed to his own
– a fact which, during the period she had borne him twelve children,
he had failed to observe. Now he was outraged: 'If we have two kings,
Sukey, we must have two beds.'

Susanna remained 'inflexible', and though she was expecting her
thirteenth child and there was very little provender in the house, the
rector went off to London. Even the birth of another daughter and the
death of King William failed to bring him back. He did not return
until the summer of 1702, when the rectory was partially destroyed by
fire after some malicious hand had tossed a firebrand on to the thatched
roof. Mr Wesley then resumed his duties, assailing his flock as fiercely

as ever. But he was reconciled with Susanna; John Wesley, born the following year, was the offspring of that reconciliation.

The lengthy absence had done nothing to endear Mr Wesley to his parishioners. In the hotly contested general election of 1705, the rector promised his support to a Colonel Whichcott as a candidate for the county of Lincoln. Whichcott had been a good friend, but when Mr Wesley heard that he was receiving support from the Dissenters, he abandoned him and went to Lincoln to cast his vote for the High Church candidates. The yokels of Epworth then serenaded the rectory by night with a concert of abuse, the blowing of rams' horns, shots, and the clattering of pots and pans. This demonstration cost the life of the Wesleys' latest child when the nurse, exhausted by the tumult, fell asleep and overlaid the baby. The two-year-old John slept through it.

The persecution of the rector did not end there. He was as usual heavily in debt, and his enemies now took advantage of his plight. A man called Pindar, a relative of Whichcott's, had him arrested at the door of his church for a debt of £30. Given a little time the parson might have raised this sum, but his enemies would not allow him even a few hours, and had him committed to Lincoln Jail. He declared that he was sorry to 'leave his lambs among wolves', adding bitterly: 'Now I am at rest in the haven where I long expected to be! A jail is paradise in comparison of the life I led before I came here. . . .'

Mr Wesley remained there for three months, occupying himself in an attempt to save the souls of his 'fellow jail-birds'. Susanna, battling with starvation in the family circle, sent him her wedding ring and all the bits of jewellery she possessed so that he could buy food. He sent them back with the comment: ''Tis only what I expected of her. 'Tis not everyone could bear these things, but I bless God, my wife is less concerned with suffering them than I in writing them.'

He wrote of his plight to John Sharpe, Archbishop of York and a Privy Councillor. Though the studious archbishop was much engrossed in diocesan history, he took prompt action. His coach suddenly appeared at the rectory door. He had come to see for himself the degree of poverty which had stricken the family of this parish priest. He saw cleanliness and order, and the dignified figure of Susanna as she taught the children and ruled over a household on the borderline of starvation. 'Tell me, Mrs Wesley, whether you ever wanted bread?' he asked.

She replied: 'My Lord, I will freely own that, strictly speaking, I never did want bread. But then, I had so much care to get it before it was eat, and to pay for it after, as has often made it very unpleasant to me. And I think to have bread on such terms is the next degree of wretchedness to having none at all.'

The archbishop left a sum of money for immediate needs, and eventually cleared the debts from his own purse and by appealing for

Dr John Sharpe, Archbishop of York, paid the Rev. Samuel Wesley's debts to secure his release from Lincoln Jail.

donations. Queen Anne herself contributed £43. To the archbishop the released parson wrote: '. . . None shall go before me in welcoming Your Lordship into everlasting habitations where you will be tried no more with my misfortunes and follies.' But when the archbishop proposed to make application to the House of Lords for a 'brief' – an authority to make public collections to relieve the Wesley family – the rector turned down the offer, observing that this would have been 'the first instance of a brief for losses by child-bearing which ever came before that honourable house'.

Mr Wesley went back to Epworth so unforgiving and full of fight that some of his well-wishers advised him to look elsewhere for a living. The archbishop himself suggested that it would be wiser to place a more amenable shepherd to serve this fierce flock. Mr Wesley, however, replied: 'I confess I am not of that mind, because I may yet do some good here; and 'tis like a coward to desert my post when the enemy fire is thick upon me. They have only wounded me yet, and, I believe, can't kill me.'

They did not kill him: but in 1709 they very nearly killed John Wesley. Susanna, whose nineteenth and last child was almost due, described what happened: 'On Wednesday night, February 9th, between the hours of eleven and twelve, our house took fire; from what cause God only knows. It was discovered by some sparks falling from the roof upon a bed where one of the children [Hetty] lay, and burning her feet. . . . Mr Wesley was alarmed by a cry of "Fire!" in the street. . . . On opening his door he found the house full of smoke, and the roof was already burnt through. He immediately came to my room (I was very ill in a separate room). . . . Then he ran and burst open the nursery door and called to the maid to bring out the children. . . . She snatched up the youngest and bid the rest follow, which they did, except Jacky. When we were got into the hall and saw . . . that the roof was on the point of falling, we concluded ourselves inevitably lost. . . . Mr Wesley had such presence of mind as to think of the garden door, out of which he helped some of the children; the rest got through the windows; I was not in a condition to climb. . . . In this distress I besought our blessed Saviour to preserve me, if it were his will, from that death, and then waded through the fire, naked as I was, which did me no further harm than a little scorching of my hands and face.

'While Mr Wesley was carrying the children into the garden, he heard the child in the nursery cry out miserably for help. . . . He several times attempted the stairs, then on fire, and found they would not bear his weight. Finding it was impossible to get near him, he gave him up for lost, and kneeling down, he commended his soul to God, and left him, as he thought, perishing in the flames. . . .'

John Wesley never forgot the rescue: 'I remember all the circumstances as distinctly as though it were but yesterday. Seeing the

room was very light, I called to the maid to take me up. But none answering, I put my head out the curtains, and saw streaks of fire on top of the room. I got up and ran to the door, but could get no further, all the floor beyond it being in a blaze. I then climbed up a chest that stood near a window. One in the yard saw me, and proposed running to fetch a ladder. Another answered, "There will not be time; but lift a light man, and set him on my shoulders." They did so, and he took me out of the window. Just then the roof fell; but it fell inward, or we had all been crushed at once. When they brought me into the house where my father was, he cried out, "Come neighbours, let us kneel down! Let us give thanks to God! He has given me all my eight children: let the house go, I am rich enough!"'

Susanna then made an exclamation which stayed with John all his life: 'Is this not a brand plucked out of the burning?' In after years he had the phrase inscribed beneath one of his portraits, and he used it twenty-seven years later to head his account of the Miss Sophy affair — thus implying to Susanna what a narrow escape it had been.

'A brand plucked out of the burning'. The rescue of the five-year-old John from a fire which destroyed Epworth rectory, 9 February 1709, held a lifelong symbolic importance for him.

Amid the trials and turmoils of her child-bearing years, Susanna never relaxed the domestic and educational disciplines which would fit her children for a cultured world, and more especially for life thereafter. The children did not play with Epworth children, nor did they go to any local school. On the day that each of them reached the age of five, serious lessons lasting for six hours began. On the very first day they were expected to learn the alphabet. All but two of them managed to do so. Daughters as well as sons became proficient in Latin and Greek, and at an early age had learned by heart a great part of the New Testament. Before midday meals and before evening prayers each child was examined by Susanna. They were to eat whatever was put before them. If any of them ate anything between meals they were 'most certainly beat'. After beatings they were expected to cry softly.

Susanna expressed her kindly but ferocious discipline in no uncertain terms: 'I insist upon conquering the will of the children betimes because this is the only strong and rational foundation of a religious education.' She interviewed each child singly on different evenings for intensive spiritual teaching. John's night was Thursday, and Thursday evenings were of special significance to him throughout his life.

Susanna's regime, with which the rector never interfered, isolated the young Wesleys not only geographically but socially. There was little play, little spontaneity, no acquaintance outside the family circle. They were happy only because they had never known anything else. They were highly educated, well mannered, fastidious over their threadbare linen. For the surviving boys, Samuel, John and Charles, Susanna's training meant that they could move on to school and university exceptionally well equipped. The daughters, who stayed on in Lincolnshire and helped the rector with his endless literary projects, looking after poultry and eventually making bad marriages, did not fare so well. Samuel the eldest, thirteen years John's senior, became a Westminster scholar in 1704 and rarely returned to the family circle. He was made an usher there, and ended his career as headmaster of Blundell's. He was the author of *Poems on Several Occasions*, a medley of hymns and humorous pieces.

John Wesley was the next to go. At the age of ten and a half he gained a place at Charterhouse School (then located in London) on a nomination from the Duke of Buckingham. He remained there for six years. Little is known about his time there. Physical hardship was not alien to him, and yet, as a junior coming from such a protected if austere home, things must have been hard. He was no good at sport but kept himself fit by walking and running. Brother Samuel reported to his father: 'Jack is a brave boy, learning Hebrew as fast as he can.' Samuel by that time was living in Dean's Yard, Westminster, where John was a frequent visitor, probably spending school holidays there.

Schooldays in London: *left*, Westminster School's College Hall, where John's elder brother Samuel was an usher (1713–33). *Below*, the Charterhouse as it was when John Wesley attended the school.

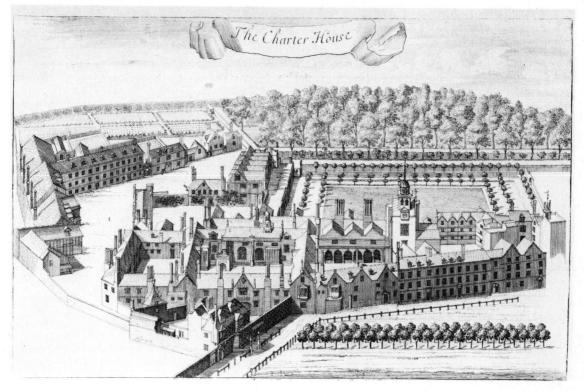

The Charter House

Dr Henry Sacheverell, rector of St Andrew's, Holborn.

On the whole Charterhouse could not have been an unhappy experience. In after years John paid friendly visits to his old school, and on one Founder's Day was one of the stewards at the annual dinner.

At the age of sixteen he considered himself ready for Oxford University. He accordingly made an approach to Dr Henry Sacheverell, a famous High Church Tory divine. In after years John described the encounter: 'I found him alone, as tall as a may-pole, and as fine as an archbishop. I was a very little fellow. . . . He said: "You are too young to go to University; you cannot know Greek and Latin yet. Go back to school." I looked at him as David looked at Goliath, and despised him in my heart. I thought: "If I do not know Greek and Latin better than you, I ought to go back to school indeed." I left him, and neither entreaties nor commands could have brought me back to him.'

It is surely at this point that John Benjamin Wesley steps out as a character in his own right after years of passive discipline. In appearance he was indeed small, almost dainty, but well proportioned. He had a natural ease and carriage in the presence of women, for whom he was a great attraction – too much so for comfort – throughout his life. He was fastidiously neat in his dress. His hair, which was naturally luxuriant, and is described sometimes as black, sometimes as auburn, he wore long. Wigs were the fashion, even for undergraduates, but he boldly asserted that he could not afford the affectation as a youth, and later saw no reason to indulge, being austere in all things. He was a great reasoner. He had sometimes infuriated his father who protested to Susanna: 'I think our Jack would not attend to the most pressing necessities of nature unless he could give a reason for it.'

He left Charterhouse in 1720, and within a week of his seventeenth birthday, with a scholarship of £40 a year, he matriculated at Christ Church. Thus he took his place in the academic life of Oxford, where he remained, apart from one break, for the next fifteen years. As an undergraduate he had a reputation for wit and disputation. He was cheerful and high-spirited, played tennis, and became a strong swimmer. He also wrote his first recorded poem – to a flea – and sent a poetic paraphrase of the Sixty-fifth Psalm to his father, who was delighted. But Susanna, who had good reason to do so, warned him: 'Make poetry sometimes your diversion, though never your business.' There was little in the demeanour of this agreeable young man to suggest that he was to be the instrument of a religious revival which would shatter the sloth and corruption inherited by the Hanoverians from the reign of Queen Anne.

Oxford University, no less than the established Church and the State, was in a period of moral decay. Adam Smith, who was there a little later than John Wesley, wrote that 'the greater part of the public professors have, for these many years, given up altogether even the

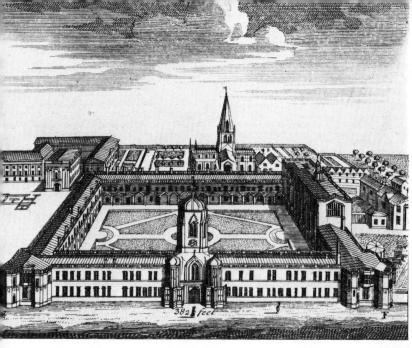

Oxford in Wesley's day: *left*, Christ Church College, which he entered as a scholar in 1720; *below left*, a view of the city, seen from St Giles; *below*, 'A drunken Fellow shocks the Vice-Chancellor', Hogarth's frontispiece for James Miller's 'The Humours of Oxford' (1730) depicts a not uncharacteristic incident of the time.

pretence of teaching'. Edward Gibbon, who spent fourteen unprofitable months at Magdalen, described the Fellows as 'easy men who supinely enjoyed the gifts of the founder. . . . Their conversation stagnated in a round of college business, Tory politics, personal anecdotes of scandal.'

Undergraduates qualified for a degree simply by being in residence for a stipulated period, and by having enough money. They frequently chose their examiners from 'their old cronies and former companions'. Nevertheless the means were there for those determined to work, and John took up his studies with characteristic diligence. Letters to and from home were theological in tone, but occasionally small anecdotes came from him. His nose began to bleed, he reported, while he was out walking. He tried every remedy to stop it. Finally he undressed and plunged into the Thames – for how long we do not know, but his nose stopped bleeding. Susanna wrote back blaming his long locks for the bleeding, and advising him to buy a wig. She was also, as ever, ready with more serious advice: 'Now, in good earnest, resolve to make religion the business of your life; for, after all, that is the one thing that strictly speaking is necessary, and all things else were comparatively little to the purposes of life.'

Wesley also reported on his spiritual state during his first year at Oxford: 'Yet I had not all this while so much as a notion of inward holiness; nay, went on habitually, and for the most part very contentedly, in some or other known sin. . . . I cannot well tell what I hoped to be saved by now, when I was continually sinning against that little light I had; unless by those transient fits of what many divines taught me to call repentance.'

Between leaving school and going up to Oxford he had not been home to Epworth, but had stayed with brother Samuel at Westminster. It was from Samuel that he learned of a new affliction at Epworth. Parish hostilities had died down after the fire, and the rectory was rebuilt as a rather more substantial brick house. But on 1 December 1716, groans and knockings were heard throughout the building. The phenomena increased in variety and volume: crashes, bangs, clatter of metal, splintering of glass. All the manifestations of a poltergeist – sometimes supposed to favour new houses. John's younger brother Charles, now nine years old, had gone to school at Westminster, so it was only the girls and a couple of living-in servants who shared the haunting with the Wesley parents. The younger children overcame their fears sufficiently to give the ghost the name of Old Jeffery. Various attempts at exorcism were made by the rector and Susanna, to no avail. A neighbouring parson, Mr Hoole, also failed in spite of his reputation as an exorcist. Finally, at the end of January 1717, Old Jeffery departed, his last knockings being heard on the outer walls of the house. The manifestations were all well documented.

The haunting of the Wesley's Epworth home was not the only well-authenticated example of the time. A near-contemporary manifestation, the Drummer of Tedworth, shared many of the same characteristics.

When John Wesley came home he made a collection of the accounts of every witness. The haunting had a profound and lasting effect upon his attitude to the supernatural, evil spirits, and ghosts, a belief he shared with Dr Samuel Johnson.

By the time he was twenty-two John Wesley's course seemed to be set, and his future predictable. He would take orders and hope for one of the livings at the disposal of the Charterhouse governors, or he might take on his father's curacy at the wretched fen village of Wroote, a scatter of hovels subject to flooding, where a thatched parsonage amid the swamps served about 200 parishioners. The only alternative was schoolmastering.

Susanna hoped for her son's return. The rector took it for granted that John would become a parson, and after serving as a curate at Wroote would take over the Epworth parish on his own retirement. All seemed set for the young man to become a country clergyman at a time when the Church of England, divided and decayed, had become little more than an appendage of the class system. Moreover, the rector himself was bringing ruin upon the household again by devoting himself to a massive and sumptuous book on Job, planned as his *magnum opus*. In furthering this project he spared no one. The daughters were put to work on cross-references, Hetty being his amanuensis until she was swept into a disastrous marriage. In London his eldest son Samuel was expected to tout for subscriptions – from Swift and Pope among others.

In the spring of 1725, the year of John's ordination, Emilia the eldest sister, grief-stricken after a broken love affair, wrote poignantly from Lincolnshire: 'Dear Brother – Whether you will be engaged to be married before thirty or not, I cannot determine; but, if my advice be worth listening to, never engage your affections before your worldly affairs are in such a posture that you marry soon. . . . I know you are a young man encompassed with difficulties . . . but believe me, if ever you come to suffer the torments of a hopeless love, all other afflictions will seem small in comparison of this.

'I know not when we had so good a year . . . but instead of saving anything to clothe my sister and myself, we are just where we were. A noble crop has almost all gone, besides the Epworth living, to pay some part of those infinite debts my father has run into, which are so many, that were he to save £50 a year, he would not be clear in the world this seven years. One thing I warn you of; let not my giving you this account be any hindrance to your affairs. If you want assistance . . . my father is as able to give it now as any time. . . .

'I have quite tired you now; pray be faithful to me. Let me have one relation I can trust. Never give a hint to any of aught I write to you; and continue to love your unhappy but affectionate sister, Emilia Wesley.'

John did indeed need assistance with his ordination fee, and the rector lurched deeper into debt as the money was being scraped together. Learning that her well-to-do brother was returning from India by a certain ship, Susanna made the long journey to London in the hope of tapping his generosity. But the brother did not appear, though the money was somehow raised when she returned empty-handed. John was ordained by John Potter, then Bishop of Oxford, subsequently Archbishop of Canterbury. Soon afterwards he preached his first sermon at South Leigh, near Witney.

This was a period of change and opportunity which eventually was to carry the young man outside the orbit of Epworth and the predictable. Within a few months of his taking orders, in March 1726, he was unanimously elected to a Fellowship at Lincoln College. This carried the right to a room in the college and a regular salary, which continued so long as he remained celibate (which meant that he benefited from it till 1751). The appointment commanded respect. Every week, besides teaching Greek, he gave lectures on passages from the Greek New Testament. He was also Moderator, directing daily

South Leigh Church

The church of South Leigh, near Witney, Oxon., where Wesley preached his first sermon after his 1725 ordination.

disputations at the university. At home the rector rejoiced: 'Wherever I am, my Jack is Fellow of Lincoln.'

With his new security John was able also to order his own studies more methodically – to use the word that would ultimately dominate his life. On Mondays and Tuesdays he studied Latin and Greek; on Wednesdays logic and ethics; on Thursdays Hebrew and Arabic; on Fridays metaphysics and natural philosophy; on Saturdays rhetoric and poetics; on Sundays theology.

Lincoln College today (*right*), and as it was when John Wesley was a Fellow. The Wesley Room (*opposite, above*), restored and furnished by American Methodists in 1926, was not John Wesley's actual lodging, which was in fact a room in Chapel Quad (*opposite, below*), where some contemporary wall paintings, here reproduced for the first time, were recently discovered.

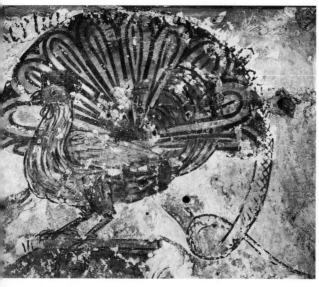

Time and the ordering of it now became something of an obsession. He grew wary of sleep as a form of self-indulgence. He set his alarm for four in the morning, and this remained his habit until old age. Small wonder that in later life he upbraided a young preacher who was sharing his room: 'Joshua, when I go to bed, I go to bed to sleep, and not to talk.'

It was in line with the new discipline that records should be kept. So he assiduously applied himself to his journal, which was intended to be public and was published in parts during his lifetime. There was also a private diary in which he used codes, shorthand, secret symbols and abbreviations. It was kept that he might be 'the better able to discharge the duty of self-examination'. This inner and secret work was not penetrated until after his death. An entry for 1725 reveals the regime he was mapping out for himself, and which was to lead him on to Methodist conceptions:

A General Rule in All Actions of Life
Whenever you are to do an action, consider how God did or would do the like, and do you imitate his example.

General Rules of Employing Time
1 Begin and end every day with God; and sleep not immoderately.
2 Be diligent in your calling.
3 Employ all spare hours in religion; as able.
4 All holidays [i.e. holy-days].

John Wesley's diary had many entries in his elegant shorthand. The left-hand column, translated in our text here, reveals his early interest in methodical and carefully ordered activity.

The Cotswold village of Stanton was at the centre of John Wesley's lively social life during the 1720s.

5 Avoid drunkards and busybodies.
6 Avoid curiosity, and all useless employments and knowledge.
7 Examine yourself every night.
8 Never on any account pass a day without setting aside at least an hour for devotion.
9 Avoid all manner of passion.

During this period he wrote to his older brother Samuel the often quoted line: 'Leisure and I have taken leave of one another.' It was a prophecy which he fulfilled later rather than a strict description of the period, for he had by now become involved in an agreeable intercourse with friends an easy ride from Oxford in the Cotswolds, a setting which contrasted pleasingly with Lincolnshire.

Wesley was introduced to this charmed circle by a jovial, pious individual, Robert Kirkham of Merton College, son of the vicar of the Cotswold village of Stanton. Robert was to become one of the first members of Charles Wesley's Holy Club, the precursor of Methodism, but he was a friend of John Wesley at least as early as 1726. Kirkham invited the brilliant young don, 'the little and handsome person', as John was described, to join his family at Stanton.

Contrast with Lincolnshire indeed! Here in a spacious comfortable vicarage, with the best of food and wine, much gaiety, social life, and conversation effortlessly turning on religion, music and literature, were Robert's three amiable, vivacious sisters. Instantly John, so much admired by Robert, was taken into the bosom of the family. This in turn led to a circle of intelligent, well-bred, affluent neighbours: Colonel Granville at Buckland, the Griffiths and the Allens at Broadway. A foible of the times among the young people of such families was the use of fanciful nicknames as a form of social intimacy. John was named Cyrus. Sally Kirkham was Varanese; Betty Kirkham was Sappho; Ann Granville was Selina; and her sister Mary was Aspasia, the dazzling Mrs Pendarves, a wealthy widow three years older than John, and destined to be described by Burke as the 'highest-bred woman in the world.'

In 1725, his critical twenty-second year, John Wesley was deeply attracted to Varanese, not for her beauty and vivacity alone but for her religious experience she shared with him. He fell in love with her with the diffidence which was a persistent strain in his character. But John contemplated marriage in the future, say six or seven years hence when he would reach his thirties. His revelation of matrimonial thoughts to his sister Emilia had caused her to write the letter already quoted. Meanwhile with Varanese it was not a courtship so much as a spiritual intimacy. The elegant young don, so much at his ease in feminine company, could dance, sing, ride and swim, but it was his fervent and articulate passion for God which brought him so close to Varanese. The intensity of their relationship owed much to her introducing him to Thomas à Kempis's *Imitation of Christ*, a work which profoundly influenced him, even though his mother in her letters tended to denigrate it. Cryptic references to Varanese appear in his private diary, and there is one reference to her which seems to indicate some declaration on his part: 'Let it not be in vain!'

It was probably very tentative, and it was in vain. Varanese's love went to another young clergyman, Jack Chapone. But they were to remain friends, and as such her significance was undiminished. 'Meeting with a religious friend, which I never till now had, I began to

A very private entry in the young Wesley's diary: in cypher is the name 'Varanese', i.e. Sally Kirkham, a lady of the Stanton circle to whom he was attracted.

26

alter the whole form of my conversation,' he wrote in his diary. But he also wrote: 'Have I loved woman or company more than God?'

He put on a brave face and danced at Varanese's wedding. His sister Emilia, always in his confidence at this time, wrote: 'Had you not lost your dear Mrs C——n, where had your love been fixed? On heaven, I hope, principally; but a large share, too, had been hers: you would not have been so spiritualized, but something of this lower world would have had its part in your heart, wise as you are; but being deprived of her there went all hope of worldly happiness: and now the mind, which is an active principle, losing its aim here, has fixed on its Maker for happiness. This will ever be the end that all rational beings will aim at, and when disappointed of one thing will soon fix on another.'

Varanese herself had no wish to drop him as a close friend. After she had been married for a year she wrote: 'I would certainly tell you, if my husband should ever resent our freedom, which I am satisfied he never will; such an accident as this would make it necessary to restrain in some measure the appearance of the esteem I have to you, but the esteem as it is grounded on reason and virtue and entirely agreeable to us both, no circumstance of life will ever make me alter.'

And later, from the security of her happy marriage (she had five children), she confessed: 'When I first saw you the utmost I desired was to take my hand round your neck. . . . I was afraid then; it was only the improbability of attaining them that made me so moderate in my wishes. I could hardly presume that you would ever condescend so far. . . . The greatest pleasures of my life, I freely own, have been owing to friendship; in the number of my friends there is no one I see, and always shall, in a stronger view than you.'

The Varanese affair did not sever him from the Cotswold circles, though in 1727 filial duty carried him back for a time to Lincolnshire. The rector, still deep in his book on Job, had had a stroke and was feeling his age. Though he was no longer at war with his parishioners he was pursued by debtors. He also had increasing difficulty in carrying out his pastoral duties in his adjacent cure of Wroote, that waterlogged fen village and its surly occupants, 'their heads as impervious as stones'. The old man had once nearly drowned trying to reach this unreceptive congregation, and the additional work was now beyond him. He needed a curate.

Samuel, the eldest son, had been approached. But he was well established in his teaching career, and declined. John, with his fellowship providing a basic income, felt obliged to go. He would be able to continue his studies while writing sermons for himself and his father, and giving some assistance to the book on Job. Accordingly, he returned home in August 1727. This was the only occasion in his life when he carried out the ordinary routines of parish priest, and he

The church of Wroote, the waterlogged village which formed part of the Rev. Samuel Wesley's Fenland parish. Here his son John acted as curate for two years (1725–7) to an unresponsive congregation.

showed little of the powers that were to come. 'From the year 1725 to 1729 I preached much, but saw no fruit of my labour,' he admitted. (John and his followers never tired of the fruit image.)

The lack of Christian charity which went with the rigours of religious discipline in the Wesley household showed itself in all its obduracy during John's two years at Wroote. His sister Hetty, who was approaching her thirtieth year and had not been without suitors, for she was lively and strikingly good-looking, fell passionately in love with a local lawyer. It could have been a good match for a girl of her age with no portion to offer, but the rector considered the young man to lack godliness, and with the concurrence of Susanna barred him from the house and forbade the match. Hetty defied them and eloped with her lover.

It is not recorded what precisely went wrong, but the young couple parted within twenty-four hours. Hetty, broken-hearted, returned home to find that Mr Wesley had forbidden even her name to be mentioned. There was no question of forgiveness. The rector devised a chilling penance – that she, regardless of her own feelings, should marry the first 'honest' man who presented himself as a candidate.

William Wright, a journeyman plumber from Lincoln – some described him as a travelling tinker – met with the Wesleys' approval and made an honest woman of poor Hetty, who wrote poetry for her brother and had been able to read the Greek Testament at the age of nine. He carried her off to London, where he set up business with the help of a £500 wedding gift from Hetty's uncle, in Frith Street, Soho, and soon took to drink. There she was to suffer from lead poisoning and to watch her children die of it. Her brothers were not indifferent to her misfortunes. Charles and Samuel visited her. John daringly preached a sermon from the parental pulpit on 'Universal Charity, or the Charity due to Wicked Persons.'

The Rector of Lincoln College, Dr Morley, wrote in October 1729 reminding John that junior Fellows who were Moderators were expected to attend personally, and that John should return to his post. All unaware of the precarious finances at Epworth, the good doctor concluded: 'Your father may certainly have another curate, though not so much to his satisfaction.'

His return to Oxford signalled a greater and lasting intimacy with his brother Charles, who had been sent to Westminster School at the age of nine, becoming a King's Scholar and eventually Captain of the school. Brother Samuel, being a housemaster, had acted as a father to the boy, and Charles never returned to Epworth during his schooling, though he kept up a voluminous correspondence. All the Wesleys wrote verse, Samuel with more of an edge to his talent than his father had shown. He was friendly with Pope, Prior and Swift, and the young Charles, himself to be the most prolific of them all, benefited from the literary society so much more liberal and less arid than Epworth. He acted in the Westminster plays and visited London theatres, which could hardly have been with the knowledge of the rector. He was gifted with a splendid singing voice. He attracted love at first sight. He was short in stature but nicely proportioned, self-assured and well able to look after himself with his wits and his fists.

While still at school a singular choice or destiny was thrust upon him. There was a wealthy branch of the Wesley family in Ireland, headed by Garrett Wesley, who had a great estate some twenty miles from Dublin. When his wife died childless, Garrett began to look about for an heir. He was a close friend of Swift, and it was perhaps through Swift's acquaintance with the Wesleys at Westminster that Garrett's eye lighted upon Charles. Here was a youth of great charm and character, highly successful at school, well mannered, gentlemanly – and penniless. He offered to adopt Charles, and gave him time to consider it.

Neither of the brothers took it upon themselves to influence the boy. Surprisingly, the rector who had not hesitated to govern the life of thirty-two-year-old Hetty made no intervention, though the Irish fortune could hardly have failed to alleviate the family plight. Without family persuasion or restraint young Charles took his time, and finally declined the offer. Why? He loved the good things of life. He had no strong ties with Epworth. He knew that he would face Oxford almost

Richard Colley and family, who benefited from Charles Wesley's idealistic rejection of the Garrett Wesley inheritance. Colley's grandson became the Duke of Wellington.

without funds. An astonishing indifference towards money seems the only explanation, borne out many years later when he married an heiress and made it a condition that her fortune should be settled on herself and go back to her family on her death. Brother John not unkindly referred to Charles's action as a 'lucky escape'. Garrett Wesley's second choice was a maternal relative, Richard Colley, grandfather of the first Duke of Wellington.

Charles arrived penniless at Oxford with an Exhibition to Christ Church in 1727 at the age of nineteen. In his middle age he described himself at this period as given to 'harmless diversions' which had kept him 'dead to God, and asleep in the arms of Satan for eighteen years.' Brother John in after years was less censorious: 'He pursued his studies diligently and led a regular harmless life; but if I spoke to him about religion he would warmly answer: "What, would you have me be a saint all at once?"'

On the face of it, the relationship between the brothers at this time seems affectionate if somewhat cool, reflecting the age gap between them. In fact a very deep and lasting bond developed at Oxford, of immense importance, in spite of conflicts, and one which profoundly affected their lives and the foundation of Methodism. John was always the acknowledged leader and the almost obsessive organizer. Charles, the poet and hymn-writer, was no less vehement than his brother, but more intuitive, more worldly, inclined indeed to be snobbish, capable

Opposite, Charles Wesley as a young man (*top left*) moved easily in the capital's literary circles, to which his brother Samuel had access. Their acquaintance included Swift (*top right*), Prior (*bottom left*), and Alexander Pope.

also of sharp criticism of the older brother's personal life. They both had the carriage and manners of gentry, and paid great attention to appearance though not to finery. They were both attractive to women. They were good musicians, with Charles playing the German flute on social occasions. When Charles arrived at Oxford he stepped into a certain amount of reflected glory, for John's talents even in the sorry and slothful state of academic life were widely recognized. While John was away at Wroote Charles, though sowing no wild oats, enjoyed college life to the full and made his own friends. But on occasion he acted in a somewhat mysterious fashion, as if he were indeed being directed toward his destiny as an evangelist. Thus he had declined the Irish fortune, and now at Oxford he had a change of heart which caused him to write to John: 'There is no one person I would so willingly have to be the instrument of good to me as you. It is through your means, I firmly believe, that God will accomplish what He hath begun in me.'

This change mystified him. In his letter he tried to explain it: 'It is owing in great measure to somebody's prayers (my mother's, most likely) that I am come to think as I do; for I cannot tell myself how or when I first woke out of my lethargy, only that it was not long after you went away.'

By the time John returned from Lincolnshire, Charles, already a Bachelor of Arts and a college tutor, had formed a modest 'club' consisting of himself, Robert Kirkham, and a consumptive Irish youth called William Morgan. They met together regularly to study the classics and to seek a serious Christian way of life. Whereas John's aspirations to godliness were private, shared between himself and his diaries, Charles cherished company on his spiritual journey. It could be said that these gatherings were the beginning of Methodism, and that Charles was actually the founder. Nevertheless, when John joined them the leadership was unanimously yielded to him. He at once laid down rules. The self-examination was to go like this:

Have I prayed with fervour . . . [every night and] Monday, Wednesday and Friday, with my friends?

Have I in private prayer frequently stopped short and observed with what fervour?

Have I duly used intercession?

1 Before.
2 After speaking to any.
3 For my friends on Sunday.
4 For my pupils on Monday.
5 For those who have particularly desired it, on Wednesday and Friday.
6 For the family in which I am, every day?

Though they were so few, their behaviour soon attracted attention and brought them, derisively, the name which would be known through the world: 'A gentleman of Merton College, who was one of our little company, which now consisted of five persons, acquainted us that he had been much rallied the day before for being a member of *The Holy Club*; . . . some men of wit in Christ Church . . . made a pretty many reflections upon the *Sacramentarians*, as they were pleased to call us. . . . It was soon reported that Dr ——— and the censors were going to blow up *The Godly Club*. . . . We were sometimes dignified with [the name] of *The Enthusiasts*, or *The Reforming Club*. . . . As for the names of *Methodists*, *Supererogationmen* and so on. . . .'

As the Holy Club, at that time the preferred title, increased in numbers and influence its obligations proliferated. Members met every evening from six till nine for prayers, psalms and study of the Greek New Testament. All their effort was devoted to leading a holy life.

The Holy Club in session: John Wesley stands at the head of the table. To his immediate right (in background) is George Whitefield. Seated at the table to Whitefield's right are James Harvey, Robert Kirkham (wearing glasses), Benjamin Ingham in conversation with Charles Wesley, and the intense and unstable William Morgan. Another of the movement's stalwarts, John Gambold, is taking down a book from the shelf at left.

Two distinguished Holy Clubmen: James Harvey (*above*) and John Gambold, who eventually left Wesley to become a Moravian bishop.

Every waking hour they prayed for several minutes, each day for a special virtue. Every Sunday they took Communion – the prescribed attendance was only three times a year. Merton College authorities actually forbade their undergraduates from weekly communion. Wednesdays and Fridays were fast days. The whole regime was devised by John, who had become aware of the value of sharing and of each man speaking out openly about his own and others' shortcomings.

Having initiated it all, Charles was happy in a subordinate position in this benevolent autocracy in which they were all equal. One new member, John Gambold, who later became a Moravian bishop, wrote: 'Mr John Wesley was always the chief manager, for which he was very fit. . . . Yet he never assumed anything to himself above his companions. Any of them might speak their mind, and their words were as strictly regarded by him as his were by them.'

When Charles visited his brother Samuel at Westminster, the profound change in his attitudes caused consternation. The liberal-minded Samuel, enjoying the freedom of literary society, was shocked at the severe Oxford regime and began to distrust John's influence. It was in fact the beginning of a rift which was to end in open hostility. Nor was he alone in his misgivings.

In 1730, William Morgan unwittingly initiated the social work of Methodism by announcing that he had been visiting prisoners in jail

Aspects of Oxford: *left*, the Bocardo
Prison, whose inmates were visited
by Wesley and other members of the
Holy Club. A container lowered by
pulley from the window above the
arch enabled passers-by to give alms
(for food) to the prisoners. *Below*,
'Scholars at a lecture', by William
Hogarth (1736/7), with the
University Registrar, Dr William
Fisher, addressing a typically
uninterested gathering.

and suggesting that the Holy Club should take up his work. The idea
was of course not new: Wesley's father and grandfather had been
prison visitors. The Holy Club responded, taking Christianity and
education to prisoners, relieving jailed debtors where possible, and also
caring for the sick and needy. For this work John Wesley sought and
obtained the blessings of his father and of the Bishop of Oxford. In his
journal he treated it all in very individual terms – a campaign for
personal holiness rather than social improvement:

'In 1730 I began visiting the prisons; assisting the poor and sick in
town; and doing what other good I could, by my presence or my little
fortune, to the bodies and souls of all men. To this end I abridged
myself of all superfluities, and many that are called necessaries of life. I
soon became a by-word for so doing, and I rejoiced that my name was
cast out as evil. The next spring I began observing the Wednesday and
Friday Fasts, commonly observed in the ancient Church; tasting no
food till three in the afternoon. And now I knew not how to go any
further. I omitted no occasion of doing good; I for that reason suffered
evil. And all this I knew to be nothing, unless as it was directed
toward inward holiness.'

In the midst of pleasure-seeking, slothful, almost heathen Oxford,
the youthful enthusiasts who followed John Wesley in self-
improvement and good works from 1730 to 1735 accepted his
discipline and the rigours that went with it. Most of them went on to

35

take orders and fade into obscurity. The consumptive William Morgan, however, had a mental breakdown and died in 1732 at home in Ireland. Morgan's father, though a friend of the Wesley family, expressed his bitterness so freely that he provoked the following letter from John:

'On Sunday last I was informed . . . that my brother and I had killed your son; that the rigorous fasting which he had imposed on himself by our advice had increased his illness and hastened his death. Now . . . as the being thought guilty of so mischievous an imprudence might make me less able to do the work I came into the world for, I am obliged to clear myself of it by observing to you, as I have done to others, that your son left off fasting about a year and a half since; and that it is not yet half a year since I began to practise it. . . .'

He concluded, 'I have now largely and plainly laid before you the real ground of all the strange outcry you have heard; and am not without hope that by this fairer representation of it . . . you may have a more favourable opinion of a good cause, though under an ill name.'

Morgan's father was not only reconciled, but was willing to commit his younger son, Richard, to the Wesleys' care in the following year, seeking Charles as his tutor, and writing to John that 'I would have him live a sober, virtuous and religious life, and to go to church and sacrament according to the statutes and customs of his college; but for young people to pretend to be more pure and holy than the rest of mankind is a dangerous experiment.'

But young Richard Morgan brought a greyhound with him to Oxford, and had worldly notions of his own. 'There is a Society of gentlemen,' he wrote in a letter home, 'consisting of seven members, whom the world calls Methodists, of whom my tutor is President. They imagine they cannot be saved if they do not spend every hour, nay, every minute of their lives in the service of God. To that end they read prayers every day in the common jail. . . . They endeavour to reform notorious whores. . . . They rise every day at five of the clock. A religious book is read all the time we are together. Though some are remarkable for eating very heartily on gaudy-days, they stint themselves by two pence meat, and a farthing bread, and a draught of water when they dine at their own expense. . . .' By becoming his pupil, he claimed, he was stigmatized with 'the name of a Methodist, the misfortune of which I cannot describe.'

When Wesley found a copy of this letter, he reported that the youth had in fact fallen from grace. 'Is he not surrounded, even in this recess, with those who are often more pernicious than open libertines? . . .'Tis true they have not yet laughed your son out of all his diligence; but how long it will be before they have, God knows.'

This row was patched up and the young man reformed, but not before John Wesley had left no doubt of the exclusive nature of the

Left, Mrs Delany, the talented and vivacious lady who as 'Aspasia' was a leading member of the Cotswold circle surrounding the Wesleys. *Above*, Aspasia's crayon drawing of another of the group, her sister 'Selina' (Ann Granville).

club in these chilling words: 'Of his being admitted into our Society (if it deserves so honourable a title) there is no danger. All these gentlemen, whom I have the happiness to converse with two or three times a week upon a religious account, would oppose me to the utmost should I attempt to introduce among them, at those important hours, one of whose prudence I had so short a trial and who was so little experienced in piety and charity.'

Meanwhile, more sociable intercourse with the Kirkham family and friends continued to play a part in Wesley's life. After the marriage of Varanese a bond developed between John Wesley and Colonel Granville's handsome and spirited daughter, Mrs Pendarves, known to the circle as Aspasia. She, her sister Selina, and the other Cotswold friends, formed a sort of idealized feminine Holy Club in which their Cyrus (John Wesley) was spiritual leader, and his brother ('Araspes') was also always welcome.

Aspasia was destined to become, as Mrs Delany, a leader of London society and an intimate of the Royal Family. Swift described her as 'fair as the moon, clear as the sun, but terrible as an army of banners', and she was popular with most of the prominent people of

Mrs Delany in old age, after a lifetime in the highest of high society, chose to underplay the influence which John Wesley had had on her when they were young.

her time. During her friendship with 'Cyrus' she was already socially and physically on the move, and the relationship between them developed by correspondence in a flamboyant style which contrasted with the austerities of the Holy Club. From London she wrote: 'Why should I be afraid of your superior understanding when I know at the same time the delight you take in not only entertaining but improving all those you converse with? Then take me into your protection. . . . You will value me less when you know how weak I am. . . . I have been at two operas and was very much delighted. I hope it is not a fault to be transported by music. If it is, I will endeavour to correct it. I am ashamed of sending you so blotted a piece of paper.'

John Wesley's letters sometimes quivered with delicate romance: 'I spent some very agreeable moments last night . . . thinking to how little disadvantage Aspasia or Selina would have appeared even in that faint light which the moon, glimmering through the trees, poured on that part of the garden in which I was walking. How little would the eye of the mind that surveyed them have missed the absent sun! What darkness could have obscured gentleness, courtesy, humility. . . .'

While Aspasia danced and gave herself more and more to the pleasures of high society, often in the company of the wealthy Irish Wesleys, Cyrus wrote delicately worded letters of caution. Her letters ceased after she had gone to Ireland, enjoyed the society at Dublin Castle and met Swift. As a very old lady in 1783 she recalled that she 'had known the Mr Wesleys – the Methodist preachers; she knew them when they were young men. . . . They were of a serious turn, and associated with such as were so. . . . That was a happy beginning, but the vanity of being singular and growing *enthusiasts* made them endeavour to gain proselytes and adopt that system of religious doctrine which many reasonable folk thought *pernicious*. Well, well! Perhaps they did some good to the common people. . . .'

At that time the Wesleys' contacts with the common people were still largely limited to charitable visits and other activities. There were none in the Holy Club, with the exception of the amazing George Whitefield (1714–70), who was to become the last member of the club, and the most influential by far (excepting the Wesleys themselves). Whitefield was brought up by his widowed mother, who ran the Bell Inn at Gloucester, and he served as a potboy while attending a local school. His talents attracted the attention of Lady Betty Hastings, the sister of the Earl of Huntingdon who became sister-in-law of another Holy Club member, Benjamin Ingham. Through her influence he became a servitor at Pembroke College, Oxford – which meant that he paid his way by carrying out menial college duties. It was there that he read Thomas à Kempis; and was deeply affected, as was John Wesley, by William Law's *Serious Call to a Devout and Holy Life*. Samuel Johnson, Whitefield's contemporary at Pembroke, was

John Wesley greeting George Whitefield, then a servitor at Pembroke College, outside the Holy Club, Oxford. An artist's impression.

much impressed by the same book, which provided 'the first occasion of my thinking in earnest of religion after I had become capable of rational enquiry.' The effect on Whitefield led him 'to pray and sing psalms twice every day besides morning and evening, and to fast every Friday, and to receive the Sacrament at a Parish Church near our College and at the Castle where the despised Methodists used to receive once a month.'

But Whitefield still found himself at a distance from the exclusive Wesleys: 'For about a twelvemonth my soul longed to be acquainted with some of them.' After helping an old woman in the workhouse who had tried to cut her throat, he was introduced to Charles Wesley in 1735 and received by the Holy Club. Only a few years later his extraordinary histrionic powers were to make him the most famous preacher of his time.

At Epworth the old rector encouraged his sons in their activities, but the time came when, at over seventy, he had to look for a successor. He appealed first to Samuel, who was well established in his teaching career and declined. Then he turned to John, who wrote at great length explaining that he could not take on the task. In the course of this he counted his present blessings in no uncertain terms:

'I know no other place under heaven where I can have always at hand half a dozen persons nearly of my own judgement and engaged in the same studies: persons who are awakened into a full and lively conviction that they have only one work to do upon earth; who are in some measure enlightened so as to see, though at a distance, what that one work is – viz. the recovery of that single intention and pure affection which were in Christ Jesus; who, in order to achieve this, have according to their power renounced themselves, and wholly and absolutely devoted themselves to God. . . .

'Freedom from care I take to be the next greatest advantage to freedom from useless and therefore hurtful company. And this too I enjoy in greater perfection here than I can ever expect to do anywhere else. I hear of such a thing as the *cares of this world*, and I read of them, but I know them not. My income is ready for me on so many stated days, and all I have to do is to count and carry it home. The grand article of my expense is food, and this too is provided without any care of mine. . . .'

Yet within months of turning down Epworth he was off to Georgia, leaving the old man to resign the parish 'to God and the Archbishop'. He died before they set sail.

One of the century's most vivid men of action, General James Edward Oglethorpe (1696–1785), translated the young Wesleys from the academic calm, spiritual advancement and localized good works which seemed set to carry them through to middle age. He was only seven years older than John. Still in his thirties, he was already a national figure, an experienced soldier, a fervent humanist, a Member of Parliament.

As a young soldier he had served in the German army and on the recommendation of Marlborough he had been appointed ADC to Prince Eugene. When he came back to England at the age of twenty-six he entered Parliament, and soon afterwards became interested in prisons. An acquaintance of his, an architect, had been imprisoned for debt. His search for this man and the discovery of the conditions in which he had starved and died of jail fever so aroused his humanitarian instincts that he made powerful pleas in Parliament and was appointed chairman of a committee to investigate debtors' prisons. As a result of the investigations in 1729 and 1730 some 10,000 debtors were set free.

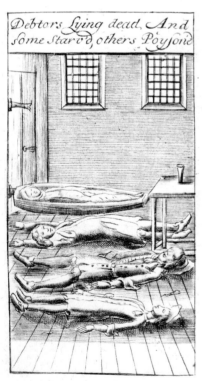

Debtors Lying dead, And some Star'd, others Poyson'd

The Fleet Prison, where the jailed debtors' dreadful conditions became a public scandal.

This set a new problem – how to cope with so many mostly homeless, penniless people. Conditions in the kingdom, especially in London, were already bad, with thousands drifting round, starving, looking for work. Oglethorpe took characteristic action both as a soldier and as a philanthropist. The British colonization of eastern America had reached a critical point where the settlers of Carolina were facing Spanish inroads from the south. As a military measure to hold the Spaniards, Oglethorpe proposed a new fortified colony. As a humanist he suggested that it should be peopled by released debtors and needy families from Britain, and by persecuted Protestants from

General J. E. Oglethorpe, moving spirit in the liberation of 10,000 debtors and their resettlement in the new colony of Georgia. A family friend of the Wesleys, in 1735 he took John and Charles with him to America.

The Creek Indian chief Tomo-Chi-Chi, brought to England by Oglethorpe in 1734 and visited by John Wesley at Lincoln. 'I went to America to convert the Indians,' Wesley later wrote, 'But, oh! who shall convert me?'

Europe. He obtained funds from the newly founded SPCK, and brought together a body of trustees to obtain a charter and found the colony of Georgia. On the board were Members of the Lords and the Commons, philanthropists, clergy and merchants. The idea of the colony was acclaimed and received widespread support, not only in money but in agricultural necessities, military equipment, and religious and educational books.

Oglethorpe led the first expedition in 1732, laid out the settlement at Savannah, made military dispositions, and won over the native Creek and Cherokee Indians. In 1734 he returned to London, bringing with him Tomo-Chi-Chi, a Creek chief, with five others. The Indians were entertained by the King, the Archbishop of Canterbury and Eton College. Their visit aroused intense excitement. They had to be protected from enthusiastic crowds determined to see and touch the 'noble savages'. When they visited Lincoln John Wesley took his sister Kezia to see them.

There were already connections between Oglethorpe and the Wesley family. Oglethorpe had subscribed to one of the old rector's books, and Mr Wesley corresponded enthusiastically about the missionary needs of the new colony, even suggesting names, though it never crossed his mind that his own sons might be candidates. Samuel, the elder brother, was one of several poets who felt moved to celebrate Oglethorpe's colonization:

> *How views the Mother Isle your little State!*
> *How aids the Senate! How the Nation loves!*
> *How George protects and Caroline approves!*

Nevertheless, he was outraged when he learnt that his two brothers were to sail away to this new Utopia. Dr John Burton, the scholar and divine who had preached the sermon which launched the fund-raising, had the task of choosing a clergyman to accompany Oglethorpe on his return to Georgia to consolidate the colony. The expense was to be met by the SPCK, and it was intended that the clergyman should be more a missionary to the Indians than a pastor for the heterogeneous flocks of settlers. It was an ill-conceived notion; Burton's choice of John Wesley as a candidate was little short of ludicrous, and the later addition of his brother was grotesque.

John's reasons for taking the appointment seem childishly naive. In the course of a letter to Burton he declared: 'My chief motive is the hope of saving my own soul. I hope to learn the true sense of the gospel of Christ by preaching it to the heathen. They have no comments to construe away the text. . . . By these, therefore, I hope to learn the purity of that faith which was once delivered to the saints. . . .'

The reason for Charles joining the venture was simply that John wished it. Dr Burton was persuaded to suggest to the governor that he

might need a second clergyman, and Oglethorpe impulsively agreed to take Charles as governor's secretary. Burton insisted that he should be ordained forthwith, an event he recalled sadly in after years: 'I took my degree, and only thought of spending all my days in Oxford. But my brother, who always had the ascendant over me, persuaded me to accompany him and Mr Oglethorpe to Georgia. I exceedingly dreaded entering into Holy Orders but he over-ruled me here also, and I was ordained deacon by the Bishop of Oxford, and the next Sunday, priest by the Bishop of London.'

The brothers, accompanied by Benjamin Ingham of the Holy Club, and by Charles Delamotte 'who had offered himself some days before', set out from Gravesend aboard the *Simmonds* on 14 October 1735, sailing with another vessel under convoy of a man-of-war. Oglethorpe was on board, with a military contingent which he drilled regularly. There was a miscellaneous and not very savoury collection of settlers, including a Mrs Welch and a Mrs Hawkins who were destined to make trouble for the Wesleys. And there was also a party of twenty-six Moravians, missionaries from Count Zinzendorf's sanctuary of Herrnhut, who were to have a profound effect upon John Wesley.

On board, the brothers carried on much of the discipline of the Holy Club, with private prayers at four in the morning, frequent services, and readings and exhortations for the settlers. John laid down

Mr Oglethorpe	
Mr Johnson	
Mr Pury	
Mrs Mackay	
2s Mr Dempsey	
Lewis Dr	
3. Francis Brooks	18
Alexander Grimaldi	49
James Billinghurst	14
John Hughes	14
4. Daniel Arthur	17
John Brownfield	21
5. David Tannerberger	39
John his Son	9
Geo. Keifer	20
Augustin Keifer	18
6. David Seisberger	39
Rosina his Wife	39
7. Judith Felathigen	29
Catherina Spidelin	30
Clara Jaskin	19
8. David Aitchman	39
Adolph Vontherndorf	29
Anne Waskin	50
9. Rosina Havenichdea	46
Richard Demustin	31
10. Jo Andrew Dover	27
Anna Catharina his Wife	20
11. William Allen	32
Eliz. his Wife	32
Frances Dr of J. Third	13
12. Rich. White	39
Will. Weston	20
13. Sam'l Davidson	35
Susanna his Wife	25
Jun his Dr 7 months	
Benjamin Goldwire	14
14. Will. Haddon	29
Jo Robinson	20
15. Tho. Hird	42
Grace, his Wife	39
Phebe, his Dr	17
16. Mark his Son	21
Jo. ditto	12
Mr Jo	
Mr C. Wesley	
Mr Ingham	
Mr Delamotte	

48 Persons.

Martha Delegrace		33
Lewis		8
Solomon		2
Sarah Harkess, her Maid		20
Wm Taverner		16
Eliz. Wheeler	Mr Horton's	26
Catherine	Mr Hawkins's	
Anne Harris	Mr Oglethorpe's	
Mary —	Do	
17. Tho. Procter		42
Eliz. his Wife		32
James his Son +		
18. Will. Do		7½
Jo. Do		3
Susannah, his Dr		5
19. Martha Tackner		40
Eliz. Hazle, her Dr		18
Do her Son		12
20. Ambrose Tackner		30
Charles Carter, Serv't to ye Trust		14
21. Jo Welch		35
Anne, his W		25
James 2 Sons		5
Jo		3
22. Robert Patterson		31
Mary 5		27
23. Samuel & Perkins		33
Catharine		26
24. Jo Walker, his L		19
Jo Cooksey, Dr Gielfair's		17
Tho. Procter's Son		16
25. Jacob Frank		31
Nathan Spanish		31
Jo Bainer		23
26. Matt. Seedbolt		20
Mathe Maack		23
27. Gottlieb Dought		19
Jo Frederick Fisher		27
Michael Meyer		21
Michael Fulmer		65
David Haach		25
29. Will. Ferris		21
Tho. Bush		33
Claudius Vanderster		33
Edmund Seaton		21
Will. Cooper		19
George Sunderland		15
30. Benj. Ward		28
Mary Ward		21

48 49

the rules, and no single waking hour was misspent. But the almost captive congregation resented the great cabin being used for prayers twice a day. 'The people,' John admitted, 'were angry at my expounding so often.'

He concentrated much religious zeal upon Mrs Hawkins, whose husband was the only doctor for the settlement, and upon her friend and fellow trouble-maker Mrs Welch, who was 'big with child'. Oglethorpe gallantly gave up his cabin to the pregnant lady, and John visited her there daily. She and Mrs Hawkins tolerated his pastoral concern and flirted with penitence and piety. Their dissimulations convinced John that he had confirmed them in a new way of life, though Charles and Ingham warned him against this. They were right of course. The ladies were chagrined when it was clear that the handsome clergyman was impervious to their advances. They became bored with him, and by the end of the voyage resentful and vindictive.

John had been studying German the better to converse with the Moravians, who lived a quiet self-sufficient life during that long stormy voyage. 'I had long observed the great seriousness of their behaviour,' he wrote in his journal. 'Of their humility they had given a continual proof, by performing those servile offices for the other passengers, which none of the English would undertake; for which they desired, and

Above, the *Simmonds*, in which John Wesley sailed to Georgia, leaving Gravesend 14 October 1735. *Opposite*, the passenger list, showing the names of the Moravians and the English settlers. Wesley's party appears at the bottom of the first column.

would receive no pay, saying, "it was good for their proud hearts", and "their loving Saviour had done more for them" . . .

'There was now an opportunity of trying whether they were delivered from the spirit of fear, as well as from that of pride, anger, and revenge. In the midst of the psalm wherewith their service began, the sea broke over, split the mainsail in pieces, covered the ship, and poured in between the decks, as if the great deep had already swallowed us up. A terrible screaming began among the English. The Germans calmly sung on. I asked one of them afterwards, "Was you not afraid?" He answered, "I thank God, no." I asked, "But were not your women and children afraid?" He replied mildly, "No; our women and children are not afraid to die."

'From them I went to their crying, trembling neighbours, and pointed out to them the difference in the hour of trial, between him that feareth God, and him that feareth Him not.'

On 6 February 1735 they set foot on American soil, pleased with 'the bloom of spring in the depth of winter'. For John there was a new lesson. Instead of converting Indians or exhorting the settlers he came under the scrutiny of the young Augustus Gottlieb Spangenburg, who had come over with the first company of Moravians. 'I soon found what spirit he was of: and asked his advice with regard to my own conduct. He said, "My brother, I must first ask you one or two questions. Have you the witness within yourself? Does the Spirit of God bear witness with your spirit, that you are a child of God?" I was surprised, and knew not what to answer. He observed it, and asked, "Do you know Jesus Christ?" I paused, and said, "I know He is the Saviour of the world." "True," replied he; "but do you know He has saved you?" I answered, "I hope He has died to save me." He only added, "Do you know yourself?" I said, "I do." But I fear they were vain words.'

Behind the vain words lay the realization that this pastor, two years younger than himself, possessed a sense of the presence of God which he lacked, a spiritual simplicity which he himself was to achieve only in time. But that spring in Savannah there was no hint that his destiny lay in moving the spirits of multitudes. His life and work were circumscribed and doomed to failure. Oglethorpe decreed that rum and slavery were prohibited in the new colony – both highly unpopular bans among settlers who, unlike those from the *Mayflower*, brought no Puritan scruples with them, and were convinced that the only way to deal with virgin land was by the labour of negroes who would stand up to the climate. (Within a few years both rum and slavery were permitted.) John Wesley had indulged his righteousness on arrival by staving in several cases of rum. This was remembered against him, and he was blamed as instigator of any of the governor's unpopular measures.

Augustus Spangenberg, the
Moravian pastor in Georgia who first
made John Wesley conscious of his
own spiritual inadequacies.

Oglethorpe also decreed that Savannah was to be John's 'parish',
while Charles went off to Frederica, some 100 miles from the coast, to
look after the settlers there and to attend him while he strengthened the
defences. The cherished notion of missionary work among the Indians
had to be relinquished. John was faced, not with innocent heathens,
but with a heathenish rabble in a parish which would have daunted a
very experienced parish priest. Oxford and a brief spell at Wroote were
no sort of preparation for this. The number of parishioners was some
700 souls, but there was no church so meetings were held in the
courthouse. There was, however, a parsonage, a roomy house on the
outskirts of the settlement with a good garden in which John
sometimes worked.

He set about his duties in his usual methodical, ritualist way. On
Sundays he held services at five, eleven and three, with prayers in
French and Italian in between and children's catechism at two. Soon 'I
began visiting my parishioners in order, from house to house; for which

The new colony of Georgia: *right*, a map of 'the inhabited part'; *below*, a contemporary plan of Savannah, showing the semi-military nature of the settlement. The hut on the middle left, marked 'F', was designated as 'the Parsonage House', while 'G' signified 'ground to build church on'.

Charles Wesley preaching to the Indians. An artist's impression.

I set apart (the time when they cannot work, because of the heat), viz. from twelve till three in the afternoon.'

At Savannah, Wesley introduced several of the practices of the Primitive Church, including total immersion of infants at baptism. When a Mrs Parker came to him with a child to be baptized, and would not consent to it being dipped he said: 'If you certify that your child is weak, it will suffice to pour water upon it.'

'Nay, the child is not weak,' Mrs Parker replied. 'But I am resolved it shall not be dipped.'

John Wesley then refused baptism.

Sunday observance was so rigidly enforced that Mrs Hawkins's husband, the only doctor in the community, was confined to the guardroom for shooting game on the Sabbath. One of his patients suffered a miscarriage owing to his absence. That the sick should suffer for the rigid enforcement of Sunday sent a wave of indignation through the settlers – directed of course towards John.

49

The trouble that Mrs Hawkins could make in a small, gossip-riddled community was to hit both brothers. John suffered direct violence. He had received a letter from Charles in which there was a reference in Greek to her and Mrs Welch. Mrs Hawkins seems to have had no difficulty in getting to know about this, openly taxed John with the Greek reference, and obtained the tactless admission that it probably referred to her and Mrs Welch. Her vengeance was terrible. A few days later she sent a servant to summon him saying she was ill. It was his pastoral duty to attend her, and he was duly admitted to her room where he was confronted not by an invalid but by a virago. Mrs Hawkins stood with her hands behind her back and shouted: 'Sir, you have wronged me, and I will shoot you through the head this moment with a brace of balls.' She then revealed a pistol in one hand and a pair of scissors in the other. The little pastor gripped her wrists, but she forced him back on to a bed, declaring that she would have his hair even if she didn't have his heart's blood. Servants, too terrified to intervene, brought in a constable who seized Mrs Hawkins but not before she had again attacked Wesley, tearing off the sleeve of his cassock with her teeth.

In Frederica things had been going even worse for Charles. As a parish priest his narrow clericalism was completely out of tune with a mainly roughneck community trying to establish a living. He summoned everybody to his daily services by drumbeat. He listened to every bit of gossip – of which there was plenty in that ill-assorted community. He taxed the patience of Oglethorpe, who was trying to concentrate all his energies on the defence of his territory against the Spaniards.

Against this background Charles fell into a trap set by the ubiquitous ladies Mrs Hawkins and Mrs Welch. They confessed penitentially to the gullible Charles that they had had intimate, perhaps adulterous, relations with Oglethorpe. Charles had observed that his master was a romantic figure in his prime, not averse to the attentions of ladies, and he therefore swallowed this fabrication. But of course the venomous ploy did not end there. Mrs Hawkins went to Oglethorpe to warn him that his secretary and chaplain was carrying on an adulterous affair with Mrs Welch.

The rift between the two men was almost complete. Oglethorpe had Charles watched, and found that he did indeed visit Mrs Welch, though it was strictly for her spiritual welfare. Charles, already unpopular, felt himself isolated and went down with a nervous fever followed by dysentery. He had no personal possessions. Abandoned by everybody except for a good Christian who brought him gruel, he lay on the mud floor of his hut, forcing himself to rise only to take services which nobody attended. Fortunately a report of his plight reached John, who hastened from Savannah. Charles, convinced that he was watched by the ungodly Oglethorpe's minions, led him into the woods and spoke in Latin, pouring out the whole story. John took immediate action. He went to Oglethorpe and persuaded him to let Charles explain himself. He undertook Charles's secretarial tasks, and put the governor's paper work to rights. He also took services on his brother's behalf. There was a reconciliation. Oglethorpe had thought of punishing Charles publicly and dismissing him. Instead: 'I considered the effect it would have on religion. That that should be wounded through your side I could not bear. Your history would be made a play or novel of.'

This was generous, but he would not keep Charles who was sent back to England as a courier – a polite exit for an unmitigated failure – with the governor's parting advice to get married.

Oglethorpe's regard for John, however, was undiminished. He wanted him to settle down to lead the religious life of the colony as the number of settlers increased. It was therefore desirable that a wife be found, and in the eyes of Oglethorpe there was no more suitable match than Miss Sophy Hopkey. She was the niece and ward of Thomas Causton, who kept a store and had been appointed chief magistrate at Savannah by Oglethorpe, in spite of a shady past of fraud in England. Causton was already a man of wealth, and Sophy was considered an heiress in Georgia. She had many suitors, but Causton and his wife were well pleased that the girl herself seemed attracted to the man of God.

Sophy now began to pay daily visits to the parsonage for prayers and French lessons, and shared John's interest in his garden. Young Charles Delamotte, who lived with and hero-worshipped John, became jealous. It became evident that Wesley was in love. When he was taken ill Miss Sophy came and nursed him. He was singularly susceptible to this motherly care, as we shall see later. She was like himself neat. She wore white dresses to please him. She spoke sparingly. Most biographers agree that she spent a lot of time just looking at him. In fact she was full of expectancy.

Wesley consulted the saintly Moravians, and came away 'amazed to the last degree' when their pastor told him he saw nothing wrong in marriage. He took himself off to the settlement of Irene, sending the girl a note: 'I find, Miss Sophy, that I can't take fire into my bosom, and not be burnt. I am therefore retiring for a while to desire the direction of God. Join with me, my friend, in fervent prayer that He would show me what is best to be done.'

Miss Sophy was not content with prayers. She had her reputation to consider. On his return she expected something explicit. Instead she heard him say, 'I am resolved, Miss Sophy, if I marry at all, not to do it till I have been among the Indians.' This was too much. Everyone had been watching her comings and goings to the pastor's house. She

A page from Wesley's journal *re* Miss Sophy Hopkey, the girl from Savannah whom he came near marrying, in which he describes her fiancé as 'a person not memorable for handsomeness, neither for gentleness, neither for wit or knowledge or sense, and least of all for religion.'

announced that she would come no more to breakfast, blameless feasts with prayers and the long-suffering Delamotte always in attendance. She soon followed this by telling him: 'I don't think it signifies for me to learn French any longer, and people wonder what I can do so long at your house.'

When he paid her a visit this ecstatic note appeared in his journal. 'Calling at Mrs Causton's she was there alone. This was indeed an hour of trial. Her words, her eyes, her air, her every motion and gesture, were full of such a softness and sweetness! I know not what might have been the consequence had I then but touched her hand. And how I avoided it I know not. Surely God is over all!'

The Caustons took some pains to show off the property that Miss Sophy would inherit and share with the right man. Thomas Causton was quite explicit. Sophy was now in Frederica, and when John

Wesley was about to go there on pastoral duty Causton said to him, 'I give her up to you. Do what you will with her. Take her into your own hands. Promise her what you will. I will make it good.'

Even the prolonged tête-à-tête of the boat journey back from Frederica failed to wring any promise from the lovesick John, who persisted in confessing himself 'much afraid'. Dalliance continued until March 1737, when it was terminated by Mrs Causton declaring: 'Sir, Mr Causton and I are exceedingly much obliged to you for all the pains you have taken about Sophy. And so is Sophy too; and she desires that you would publish the banns of marriage between her and Mr Williamson on Sunday. . . .'

John demanded and obtained a private interview with the girl. Williamson said, 'I suppose, sir, you know what was agreed on last night between Miss Sophy and me?' Wesley replied, 'I have heard something, but I could not believe it unless I should hear it from Miss Sophy herself.'

Williamson withdrew. But following the interview he made it clear that he had had enough. He sought out Wesley and said: 'Sir, you shall speak to her no more till we are married. You can persuade her to anything. After you went from the lot yesterday she would neither eat nor drink for two hours, but was crying continually and in such an agony she was fit for nothing.'

Wesley had already refused to perform a wedding ceremony for a couple who did not conform to his rigorous High Church standards. He turned people away from the communion table for similar reasons just as his father had done. It was not surprising, therefore, that on 12 March 1737 Miss Sophy and William Williamson, together with another couple whose spiritual credentials were in some doubt, travelled across the border into Carolina to be married by a pastor at Purrysburg. It was exactly a year since he had first set eyes on Miss Sophy.

For the rest of that spring and summer of 1737 Wesley, broken-hearted to the extent of losing his judgment, continued his rigorous pastoral duties, lonely and unpopular. He was vexed that Miss Sophy (he continued to write of her as such) was becoming lax in her religious enthusiasm. He reproached her for not attending prayers at five o'clock in the morning. Then, on Sunday, August 7, 'I repelled Mrs Williamson from the Holy Communion, for the reasons specified in my letter of July 5, as well as for not giving me notice of her design to communicate after having intermitted it for some time. . . . I foresaw the consequences well.'

The consequences were devastating. On the Monday Causton obtained a warrant for Wesley's arrest for defamation of the character of Mrs Williamson. He appeared in court and was permitted to leave without bail when the judge announced 'Mr Wesley's word is sufficient.' At the next session a great list of complaints against him were tabulated before a jury of forty men. As the case dragged on he continued to hold prayer meetings and services. Notices went up in Savannah restraining him from leaving the town and forbidding anyone to help him. He was found guilty on some counts but on others he held out, claiming that the court had no jurisdiction over ecclesiastical matters. Oglethorpe was away in England. Clearly Wesley had no future in America. Throughout his life he never lacked courage. His decision to flee was a brave one. It entailed a hazardous journey through jungle conditions and picking up a boat to take him to Charleston. There the faithful Delamotte met him with his papers and his few possessions, and some money. There was just enough for the passage, and he sailed over Charleston Bar for England on Christmas Eve 1737. He never returned to America though his influence was to be vital in the establishment of American Methodism. In modern Savannah a square is named in his honour.

On 1 February 1738 he reached Deal and learned that George Whitefield had left for America the day before, largely through his own appeal for help in the new colony. The impact of Whitefield on America was to be immediate and significant for, young as he was, Whitefield had already risen to full stature as a preacher.

For John Wesley the ordeals of the body and of the affections were over for the time being. This year of 1738 marked a supreme ordeal of the spirit, culminating in his conversion. On January 24, while still on board ship, he wrote in his journal:

'I went to America to convert the Indians! But, oh! who shall convert me? Who, what is he that will deliver *me* from this evil heart of unbelief? I have a fair summer religion. I can talk well – nay, and believe myself, while no danger is near, but let death look me in the face, and my spirit is troubled.'

The searching self-enquiry continued on the day of his arrival in England, when he wrote, 'I, who went to America to convert others, was never myself converted to God.' His learning, eloquence, good works, renunciation, austerities – all were 'dung and dross' without that 'sure trust and confidence in God, that, through the merits of Christ, my sins are forgiven, and I reconciled to the favour of God.' This was the faith whose lack he now felt so desperately. Earlier he had thought he 'was to lay his bones at Oxford', resuming his life as scholar, priest, and perhaps head of a new Holy Club. But now he was painfully aware of the limitations imposed by his dogmatism.

Charles, meanwhile, had enjoyed something of a hero's return, received by bishops, archbishops, by the King himself, and not least by Varanese and Aspasia. He had tried to revive the Holy Club without success, and was now somewhat at a loose end. He talked airily of

The Moravian pastor Peter Boehler, instrument of John Wesley's eventual conversion on his return to England, 1738.

returning to America but had become very restless, and this affected his health. John for his part reported to Oglethorpe and the Trustees, and settled everything on amicable terms. If Oglethorpe felt let down by the brothers he showed no sign of it, and remained a family friend until they were all old men together.

But the spiritual crisis persisted. Within five days of reaching London John had another very significant encounter with a Moravian, the young pastor Peter Boehler. Boehler, like Spangenburg in Georgia, immediately identified Wesley's condition as a lack of Saving Faith, of personal belief in salvation. The two men went to Oxford together, where Boehler told him, 'My brother, this philosophy of yours must be entirely purged away.' The Moravian's words tallied with Wesley's own self-questionings, and now, 'clearly convinced of unbelief', he asked whether he should abandon preaching:

'He answered, "By no means." I asked, "But what shall I preach?" He said "Preach faith till you have it; and then, because you have it, you will preach faith." Accordingly, Monday 6 [of March], I began

Cup used at the love-feasts of the early Methodists, shared in token of brotherly and sisterly love, as among the early Christians.

preaching this new doctrine, though my soul started back from the work. The first person to whom I offered salvation by faith alone was a prisoner under sentence of death. His name was Clifford. Peter Boehler had many times desired me to speak to him before. But I could not prevail on myself to do so; being still (as I had been many years) a zealous assertor of the impossibility of a death-bed repentance.'

So Wesley, while still seeking the experience of vital faith for himself, now began to preach the gospel of justification by faith alone. In May a religious society was founded (on Boehler's advice) which could almost be regarded as the first Methodist group, being eventually established in Fetter Lane, London. The simple rules were laid down by Wesley: members met on Wednesdays to pray together and exhort each other; every fourth Sunday was fixed as a day of intercession; every fifth Sunday there was a general 'love-feast'. There was no question of any breakaway from the established Church.

During that month of May John Wesley was constantly preaching the new message in London churches – but always through his exuberance falling foul of the Establishment. 'I preached at St Laurence's in the morning; and afterwards at St Katherine Cree's Church. I was enabled to speak strong words at both; and was therefore the less surprised at being informed, I was not to preach any more in either of these churches.' Then at St Helen's: 'My heart was now so enlarged to declare the love of God to all that were oppressed by the Devil, that I did not wonder in the least, when I was afterwards told, *Sir, you must preach here no more.*' After that six more churches banned him. It was the beginning of the nationwide Anglican opposition which was to drive him into the open air.

May 24 was the culminating point in that significant month, and it is best described in Wesley's own words: 'I think it was about five this morning, that I opened my Testament on those words. . . . "There are given unto us exceeding great and precious promises, even that ye should be partakers of the divine nature." Just as I went out, I opened it again on those words, "Thou art not far from the kingdom of God." In the afternoon I was asked to go to St Paul's. The anthem was, "Out of the deep have I called unto Thee, O Lord: Lord, hear my voice." . . .

'In the evening I went very unwillingly to a society in Aldersgate Street, where one was reading Luther's preface to the Epistle to the Romans. About a quarter before nine, while he was describing the change which God works in the heart through faith in Christ, I felt my heart strangely warmed. I felt I did trust in Christ, Christ alone for salvation; and an assurance was given me that He had taken away *my* sins, even *mine*, and saved *me* from the law of sin and death.

'I began to pray with all my might for those who had in a more especial manner despitefully used me and persecuted me. I then testified openly to all there what I now first felt in my heart. But it was not long before the enemy suggested, "This cannot be faith; for where is thy joy?" Then was I taught that peace and victory over sin are essential to faith in the Captain of our salvation; but that, as to the transports of joy that usually attend the beginning of it, especially in those who have mourned deeply, God sometimes giveth, sometimes withholdeth them, according to the counsels of His own will.'

Thus he recalled his 'conversion'. It turns on the difficult concepts of faith and grace; also on the definition of the word 'Christian'. He had begun to feel that his faith was not wholehearted, that he was not in a state of grace, after his period in Georgia. Even before, he had seen that the Moravians were able to face the prospect of death at sea without fear. He had recognized that Spangenburg had had an inner experience of the Christian faith about which he knew nothing. He had been educated to accept, and he continued to accept throughout his life (in a rational manner, being an exceptionally rational human being) the doctrines and ritual of the Church of England. But he had not felt, in his heart, the joy of surrender to Christ which he recognized

Aldersgate Street, the scene of John Wesley's conversion. Two rival sites claim the honour of being the actual place: Trinity Hall, Little Britain, and Hall House, Nettleton Court, with the balance of evidence just in favour of the latter.

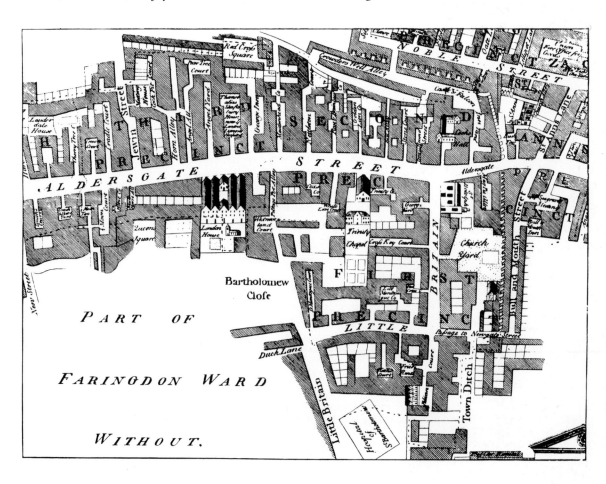

57

as the foundation of the quietism and simplicity of the Moravians' way of life. This he now strove for. It is possible that he never attained it, that the 'warmth in his heart' was a release from all the weariness of his spiritual quest. Who knows? For conversion, unless intellectual, is necessarily mystic, a psychological condition akin to that of the poet's moment of inspiration, the lover's ecstasy. Certainly there was an immediacy about his experience which convinced him that, until that moment, he had not truly been a Christian. But he had felt no divine joy, and he guessed that his experience had not therefore been complete.

One effect was to impel him towards an even more demanding regime. He resumed his 'methods', earnestly seeking for personal holiness, devoting himself to his ministries with even greater ardour. In his rational way, Wesley tidied up his experience in a measured statement that a Christian was one who had been converted and had received assurance of salvation. This emphasis on the immediacy of salvation had the inevitable corollary that faith was given to simple folk, and sinners too, as readily as to the educated searcher after truth. Such beliefs, and the new-found enthusiasm with which he preached them, held an implicit threat to the authority of the Church; but it was not one which he ever had any wish to implement. In the moment of conversion he had been *convinced* rather than *saved*. Convinced of his mission to renew the ideal of the early, primitive Church; and with no thought of creating a new one.

Charles had had a similar experience of conversion three days before John, Whitefield even earlier. John's behaviour immediately after his conversion alarmed some of the faithful, particularly the Huttons in whose house Wesley had lodged for a few days on his return from Georgia. On May 28 Mrs Hutton wrote to Samuel, the older brother, by this time headmaster of Blundell's School: 'Without ever acquainting Mr Hutton with any of his notions or designs, when Mr Hutton had ended a sermon of Bishop Blackhall's, which he had been reading in his study to a great number of people, Mr John got up and told the people that five days before he was not a Christian. . . . Mr Hutton was much surprised at this unexpected injudicious speech; but only said, *Have a care, Mr Wesley, how you despise the benefits received by the two Sacraments.* I not being in the study when this speech was made, had heard nothing of it when he came into the parlour to supper, where were my two children, two or three other of his *deluded followers* . . . and two or three gentlemen of Mr John's acquaintance, though not got into his *new notions.* He made the same wild speech again, to which I made answer – *If you was not a Christian ever since I knew you, you was a great hypocrite, for you made us all believe you was one.*'

Samuel wrote back: 'I heartily pray God to stop the progress of this lunacy.'

Opposite, John's elder brother Samuel (*top left*), now headmaster of Blundell's School, Tiverton – the letterhead (*below*) was designed by Hogarth, 1726 – was not impressed by the conversion of his younger brothers. *Top right,* James Hutton, in whose house the scandal first broke.

IN PATRIAM POPULUMQUE FLUXU

UTRIQUE UNUS   EX UNO STEMM   SURGIT HONOS

The Moravians had so impressed John that he now set out to visit the source of their work in Germany. Their sect, founded in Bohemia in 1457, had been revived by Count Zinzendorf whom Wesley, accompanied by Ingham, met at Marienborn after an exhausting journey. He then went on to the Moravian colony of Herrnhut, where he found piety and industry, an attitude of surrender to faith. The good life was untrammelled by dogma. When he left he wrote: 'I would gladly have spent my life here; but my Master calling me to labour in another part of His vineyard, I was constrained to take my leave of this happy place.'

For the first time, however, he began to have certain reservations about the Moravians, and pointed out some shortcomings in a letter he wrote but did not despatch to Herrnhut. He did not care, he said, for the Count's air of patronage. He wondered if they were not too complacent and of too closely reserved a temper. But the example of the community certainly fired him with new energy. He threw himself into active acceptance of his Master's call, with no knowledge yet of the size and extent of this part of 'His vineyard'.

On his return he preached his new theme of conscious salvation in churches all over London and in the vicinity of Oxford. He devoted much energy to the embryonic Methodism of the Fetter Lane Society, which now numbered thirty-two members. He visited prisons, and, accompanied by Charles (who addressed the crowds), he attended an execution to comfort the condemned man. Charles was with him in spirit and in action, but also celebrating in song. In his poetic rapture he even identified himself with the famous brand plucked from the burning:

> *Where shall my wondering soul begin?*
> *How shall I all to heaven aspire?*
> *A slave redeemed from death and sin,*
> *. A brand plucked from eternal fire,*
> *How shall I equal triumphs raise*
> *Or sound my great Deliverer's praise?*

Significantly his poetic flights broke clean away from the academic confines of the Holy Club:

> *Outcasts of men, to you I call,*
> *Harlots, and publicans, and thieves!*
> *He spread His arms to embrace you all,*
> *Sinners alone His grace receives:*
> *No need of him the righteous have;*
> *He came the lost to seek and save.*

After their Georgian experiences the Wesley brothers felt the need to reach out beyond the circumscribed confines of church and private society. They were not looking for social reform, though they were

Above, the Moravian colony of Herrnhut, in East Germany, which Wesley visited in 1738. *Below*, Count Zinzendorf in London, depicted with George II (on his left) and other notables on the occasion of an Act of Parliament granting special exemptions for Moravian colonists in America.

A Methodist minister exhorts the condemned man to repentance in Hogarth's 'Idle 'Prentice executed at Tyburn' (1747), while in the carriage ahead sits the officiating Anglican clergyman, at ease and aloof. On the right Hogarth has put in the 'pious bawd' Mother Douglas, sipping gin with her girls in another carriage.

willing to give spiritual comfort to whose who were victims of the brutalities of the times. They moved in a world where 160 different crimes were punishable by death. A destitute woman with a child at her breast could be hanged for taking a piece of cloth in a shop even though, finding herself observed, she had put it back. England was drinking half a million gallons of gin a year, every sixth house in London selling spirits. Prime Minister Walpole wrote to a friend, 'There is scarcely a Member whose purse I do not know to a sixpence, and whose very soul I could not purchase at the offer.' The Archbishop of Canterbury travelled in a coach with six horses and kept a state barge on the Thames, attended on land and water by a host of servants in livery. Well-placed clergymen, often the younger sons of noble families, possessed themselves of a plurality of livings, employing some wretched curate at starvation wages to do the parochial work. The Wesleys, themselves well connected, though without land or money, moved as gentry, highly educated clergymen in this uncouth world where few people could read or write. They were against drunkenness and they were for educating the common people. But they were resolutely loyal to the established Church, which they sought to reimbue with the early Christian spirit. They were not protesting at the conditions of the times, but set out to ease the burdens of those who suffered by teaching them that they were the children of God, whatever miseries or deprivations they endured.

The shocking condition of the poor people of London: 'Gin Lane' by Hogarth (1750/1) depicts violence, suicide, murder, death by starvation. The steeple of St George's, Bloomsbury, may be seen in the distance.

Such was the nature of the vision of John the methodical organizer, and of Charles the poet hymn-writer. The catalyst was George Whitefield, who returned from his American mission in December 1738. He had been popular among the colonists, founding an orphanage in Savannah, and had been pressed to return. He at least did not regard John Wesley's sojourn there as a failure. From Savannah he had written: 'The good Mr John Wesley has done in America, under God, is inexpressible.'

Whitefield had acquired a powerful reputation as a preacher even before he left for America, and this was extended on his return until, at the age of only twenty-five, he was the most famous preacher in England. There were many, including Dr Johnson, who distrusted his vehement and emotive style: 'His popularity,' said Johnson, 'is chiefly owing to the peculiarity of his manner.' But others, including Lord Chesterfield, Garrick and even Horace Walpole, were much impressed. Fashionable society and people of wealth were attracted by his dynamic preaching. His greatest patron was Selina, Countess of Huntingdon, whose sister-in-law had married Benjamin Ingham of the Holy Club.

Now, during his next few months in England, it was Whitefield who took the lead and brought John Wesley to his true vocation. Following a lightning tour of London, as a result of which he was barred from every London pulpit by the end of January 1739,

George Whitefield, the most famous and the most 'enthusiastic' of all the Methodist preachers, subsequently broke with Wesley to take a Calvinist position. His theatrical style of preaching fascinated the rich and aristocratic as well as working people. Wesley himself adopted a simpler style.

Whitefield went to Bristol. But there too the churches soon closed their doors to him. The fact that neither he nor the Wesleys betrayed the slightest disloyalty to the great, lethargic body of the established Church was not considered. It was their 'enthusiasm', and the very strength of their message that was feared, distrusted and banned from the pulpits.

Towards the end of February George Whitefield began to preach in the open to the coal miners on Kingswood Common, a few miles from Bristol. The miners of Kingswood were regarded as depraved savages, yet Whitefield's meetings drew them in ever larger numbers. Tears ran down their blackened faces, so moved were they not only by the message and the emotional eloquence of the young preacher, but also by the fact that anyone should concern himself with outcasts such as they. Whitefield went on to hold further open-air meetings at Kingswood, and also in and around Bristol, with congregations

'Credulity, superstition and fanaticism': Hogarth's satire on Methodism depicts a scene in which a thermometer records the congregation's reactions, ranging from Suicide and Madness, through Lust, to Raving. *Above*, a detail from his first version, dedicated to the Archbishop of Canterbury but never published, shows interesting differences.

sometimes swelling to 20,000, and his appeal extended to people of every kind. Within a very few months he had created a religious revival of unparalleled force throughout the populous area around Britain's second largest port.

But Whitefield was anxious to extend the work, and had also pledged himself to return to his mission in Georgia, and to bring the funds he had collected for the orphanage there. How could he leave the awakened multitude at Bristol without a pastor? In his eyes John Wesley was the one and only man to lead a religious campaign on this scale, to organize it before it became out of hand, in fact to *methodize* it. So he sent an urgent plea for John Wesley to come and take his place.

This plea caused consternation in the Fetter Lane Society. John himself was perplexed and undecided. Charles was vehemently against it. They tried opening the Bible at hazard and received no guidance. Then they had recourse to drawing lots, and by this weird

Bristol, where Methodism first took root: *right*, a view of the Dockland area; *below*, the glasshouses, site of John Wesley's early field-preaching.

method arrived at the decision that it was God's will that John should go. Charles wrote: 'We dissuaded my brother from going to Bristol, from an unaccountable fear that it would prove fatal to him. A great power was among us. He offered himself willingly to whatsoever the Lord should appoint. The next day he set out, commended by us to the grace of God. He left a blessing behind. I desired to die with him.'

No time was wasted. John reached Bristol on Saturday, 31 March 1739, and on the following day witnessed Whitefield in action: 'I could scarce reconcile myself at first,' he wrote, 'to this strange way of preaching in the fields, of which he (Whitefield) set me an example on Sunday; having been all my life (till very lately) so tenacious of every point relating to decency and order, that I should have thought the saving of souls almost a sin if it had not been done in a church.'

Thus by means of a holy lottery, and the powerful enthusiasm of young Whitefield, John Wesley at the age of thirty-six diffidently entered into the work which was to spread his renown throughout the world till, two and a half centuries later, there were more than 20,000,000 full members of the Methodist Church.

Between March and June Wesley remained in Bristol using his two great gifts – preaching and organizing. His first preaching in the open air occurred two days after his arrival. He stood on a little eminence in a brickyard and some 3,000 people gathered to hear him. Unlike Whitefield, the wild-eyed emotional evangelist, Wesley preached with simple deliberation, yet with a power that went straight to the hearts of the people. Without delay he began to form societies to give the movement a backbone of discipline. The first of these were founded in Nicholas Street and Baldwin Street. Land on the site of the Horse Fair was acquired for the first Methodist meeting house.

From the outset hostility awaited him. Whitefield's attention to the Kingswood miners had already aroused the *Gentleman's Magazine*: 'The Industry of the inferior People in a Society is the great Source of its Prosperity. But if one Man, like the Rev. Mr Whitefield, should have it in his Power, by his Preaching, to detain five or six thousands of the Vulgar from their daily Labour, what a Loss, in a little Time, may this bring to the Publick! For my part, I shall expect to hear of a prodigious Rise in the Price of Coals about the City of *Bristol*, if this Gentleman proceeds, as he has begun, with his charitable Lectures to the Colliers of *Kingswood*.'

Bringing spiritual hope to the masses was considered as dangerous as educating them. Gin, illiteracy and hopelessness in that century of wit and manners were the effective means of keeping the people in their place. As to the Church, even one of the less reactionary leaders, Dr Butler, Bishop of Bristol, attacked Wesley: 'Sir, the pretending to extraordinary revelations and gifts of the Holy Ghost is a horrid thing; yes, Sir, it is a very horrid thing. Sir, you have no business here; you are

John Wesley inaugurated a system of Society Tickets, for which members contributed one penny per week into a common fund. These groups were in effect spiritual cooperatives. The idea was later adopted by the Countess of Huntingdon's Connection, a Calvinist variant.

Richard 'Beau' Nash, the 'noted man' of Bath who tried and failed to have Wesley discredited when he came to the city (1739).

not commissioned to preach in this diocese: therefore I advise you to go hence.' Undeterred, Wesley went on preaching, enlarging his territory towards Bath where he experienced hostility of a grotesque kind. 'There was great expectation of what a noted man was to do to me there; and I was much entreated not to preach. . . .'

The noted man was Richard Nash (1674–1762) the Carmarthen Grammar school boy who became a professional gambler and attached himself to the fashionable resort of Bath. Here, as Beau Nash, he personified the arrogance and depravity of the fashionable society of the age. No doubt he had let it be widely known that he would confront the upstart preacher. Wesley noted that among the large audience were 'many of the rich and great'. He was telling them that his message was for high and low, rich and poor, when way was made for Beau Nash in all his finery. 'Coming close to me, he asked by what authority I did these things.'

'By the authority of Jesus Christ,' Wesley answered.

'This is contrary to Act of Parliament: this is a conventicle.'

'Sir, the conventicles are seditious meetings: but this is not such.'

Nash contradicted him, then went off on another tack: 'Your preaching frightens people out of their wits.'

'Sir, did you ever hear me preach?'

'No.'

'How then can you judge of what you never heard?'

'Sir, by common report.'

'Common report is not enough. Give me leave, sir, to ask, is not your name Nash?'

'My name is Nash.'

'Sir, I dare not judge of you by common report: I think it is not enough to judge by.'

Nash was at a loss, then, to try to carry off his discomfiture, declared: 'I desire to know what this people comes here for.'

From the crowd came a voice: 'Sir leave him to me: let an old woman answer him. You, Mr Nash, take care of your body; we take care of our souls: and for the food of our souls we come here.'

All this was noted in Wesley's journal, including the sting in the tail of his sermon to members of this unusual congregation: 'I do not expect that the rich and great should want either to speak with me, or hear me; for I speak the plain truth, – a thing you hear little of, and do not desire to hear.'

Significantly, this pioneer Bristol visit produced men, mostly young, who became lay preachers capable of holding together the 'societies' and 'bands' initiated by Wesley. Howell Harris from Trevecca, John Cennick from Reading, and a Bristolian, Thomas Maxfield, were among the first. This strengthened the organization Wesley

Two early Methodist field-preachers, John Cennick (*left*) and Thomas Maxfield. The years of itinerancy were now beginning, as Wesley, persuaded by his mother, delegated wide powers to the young men who followed him.

Open-air meeting at Upper Moorfields, with St Luke's Hospital in the background. This commonland just outside the City saw some of the largest early Methodist mass meetings, though the contemporary attendance figures are unreliable. The attendance at this meeting, at least, seems to have been sparse.

left behind in June 1739, when he felt obliged to return to London, 'our brethren in Fetter Lane being in great confusion for want of my presence and advice'.

Whitefield had recently returned to London. He had not been back twenty-four hours before he was preaching to 15,000 people on Kennington Common. A few days later he preached 'at a place called Mayfair, near Hyde Park Corner', to a concourse estimated at 80,000. At Moorfields, then a public park for Londoners, he regularly drew congregations numbered in thousands.

These and all attendance estimates are taken from contemporary records, often those of Wesley himself. Who counted heads is not known, but even early Methodist historians suggest that the figures should be divided by ten.

Immediately John Wesley reached London, Whitefield whisked him away to Blackheath, where 12,000–14,000 people had congregated. To Wesley's surprise, Whitefield asked him to preach in his stead, 'which I did, though my nature recoiled'. He was 'greatly moved with compassion for the rich that were there. . . . Some of them seemed to attend, while others drove away their coaches from so uncouth a preacher.'

While Whitefield was an acknowledged spellbinder, attracting people to travel miles for just a sight of him, John Wesley was deliberate, unrhetorical, not in any way extravagant. John Nelson, a stonemason from Birstall, Yorkshire, who was himself to become an important lay preacher, had listened with admiration to Whitefield: 'Mr Whitefield was to me as a man who could play well on an instrument, for his preaching was pleasant to me, and I loved the man, so that if anyone offered to disturb him, I was ready to fight for him. But I did not understand him, though I might hear him twenty times, for aught I know.'

John Nelson's response to Wesley himself, whom he heard make his first address at Moorfields, was altogether more profound: 'Oh! that was a blessed morning for my soul! As soon as he got up upon the stand, he stroked back his hair and turned his face towards where I stood, and I thought he fixed his eyes on me. His countenance struck such an awful dread upon me before I heard him speak, that it made my heart beat like the pendulum of a clock, and when he did speak, I thought his whole discourse was aimed at me. When he had done, I said, "This man can tell the secrets of my heart." . . .'

John Nelson, the artisan lay preacher from Yorkshire. Wesley's refusal to recruit preachers only from his own class was especially disliked by the Establishment.

Wesley's deliberate, unemotional magnetism produced, much more than Whitefield's emotive appeals, violent reactions in the field-preaching of these early years. At Wapping, for instance, 'many of those that heard began to call upon God with strong cries and tears. Some sank down, and there remained no strength in them; others exceedingly trembled and quaked; some were torn with a kind of convulsive motion. . . . I have seen many hysterical and many epileptic fits; but none of them were like these.'

Wesley's views on such conversions were reserved. They moved him, but they also worried him because of the offence they could give, and indeed the harm they could do, in making Methodism seem hysterical. Nevertheless, these ecstatic convulsions were frequent among people of both sexes and all ages during the first two years of Wesley's preaching. Afterwards, as his word spread throughout the country, such violent conversions became much rarer.

That same year of 1739 saw him back in the West Country, and paying his first visit to South Wales. His itineraries had begun. However, the crisis in the Fetter Lane Society which had first brought him back from Bristol was still unresolved. The Moravians in the society, led by Pastor Molther from Jena, held that until an aspirant 'knew' that his sins were forgiven, he should only 'be still' and wait for God to save him. They disliked what they saw as the aggressively salvationist tactics of the Wesleys, and resented John's apparent assumption of leadership. The final parting came in July 1740, when Wesley, having been informed that he could no longer preach in the Fetter Lane room, listed the points of disagreement. He concluded: 'I have borne with you long, hoping you would turn. But as I find you more and more confirmed in the error of your ways, nothing now

The New Room, Bristol, showing the preacher's stable, with a statue of Wesley on horseback. This was the first Methodist meeting-house, built on the site of the Horse Fair.

remains but that I should give you up to God. You that are of the same judgement, follow me.'

In the same year, the breach between Wesley's Methodism and Whitefield's Calvinism became increasingly evident, and relations between the two leaders were strained almost to breaking point. 'No scripture can mean that God is not love,' Wesley had said in his famous sermon on Free Grace, 'or that his mercy is not over all his works; that is, whatever it proves beside, no scripture can prove predestination.' It was Wesley's gospel of the universal love of God which caused his rupture with Calvinism, and though the friendship between the two men was renewed, Whitefield's adherents remained outside Wesley's influence.

Following the split with the Moravians, eighteen or nineteen of the members of the Fetter Lane Society left with Wesley. There was now an urgent need for a focal point in London, corresponding to the meeting house established at the Horse Fair at Bristol. During the unusually cold winter of 1739 he had been invited to preach in a large disused building near Moorfields, 'which had been the King's Foundery for Cannon'. It had been derelict for over twenty years. Cannon captured from the French in the campaigns of Marlborough

The New Room, Bristol, interior of the Chapel (*left*), and Wesley's room (*below*).

The Foundery, a damaged building which became Methodism's first London headquarters: 'A' indicates John Wesley's apartment, 'B' his study, 'E' the chapel entrance, 'F' a dwelling house for family preachers, 'G' a room used as a school, band room, etc., and 'H' the stable.

Opposite, plan of Moorfields, where Methodism began to establish itself round the area of the Foundery.

had been brought there in 1716 for recasting. Crowds had gathered to watch, in spite of a warning given by a young Swiss, Andrew Schalch, who detected humidity in the moulds. The Surveyor-General of Ordnance ignored this, and a contemporary account reported: 'The furnaces being opened, the fluid metal rushed into the moulds, the moisture in which was instantly converted into steam, and its expansive force, acting upon the metal, drove it out in all directions with extreme violence. Part of the roof was blown off, the galleries gave way, and a scene of serious mischief and distress followed. Many of the spectators had their limbs broken, most of the workmen were burnt in a dreadful manner, and several lives were lost.' This building, restored, was to be the headquarters of Methodism until 1778, when the City Road Chapel was opened.

Wesley's only income was the £28 a year from his Fellowship at Oxford. He had assumed heavy financial liabilities over the meeting house at Bristol. He now used £115 to buy the lease of the Foundery. Another £700 was needed for repairs and alterations. Subscriptions and loans brought in enough to provide a rough-and-ready chapel to hold 1,500. Behind this was a band room to accommodate 300, one end of it being used as a school. Above were living rooms for Wesley – he never had a conventional home – and accommodation for his widowed mother Susanna in her declining years. The need for mobility was already recognized by the provision of stabling.

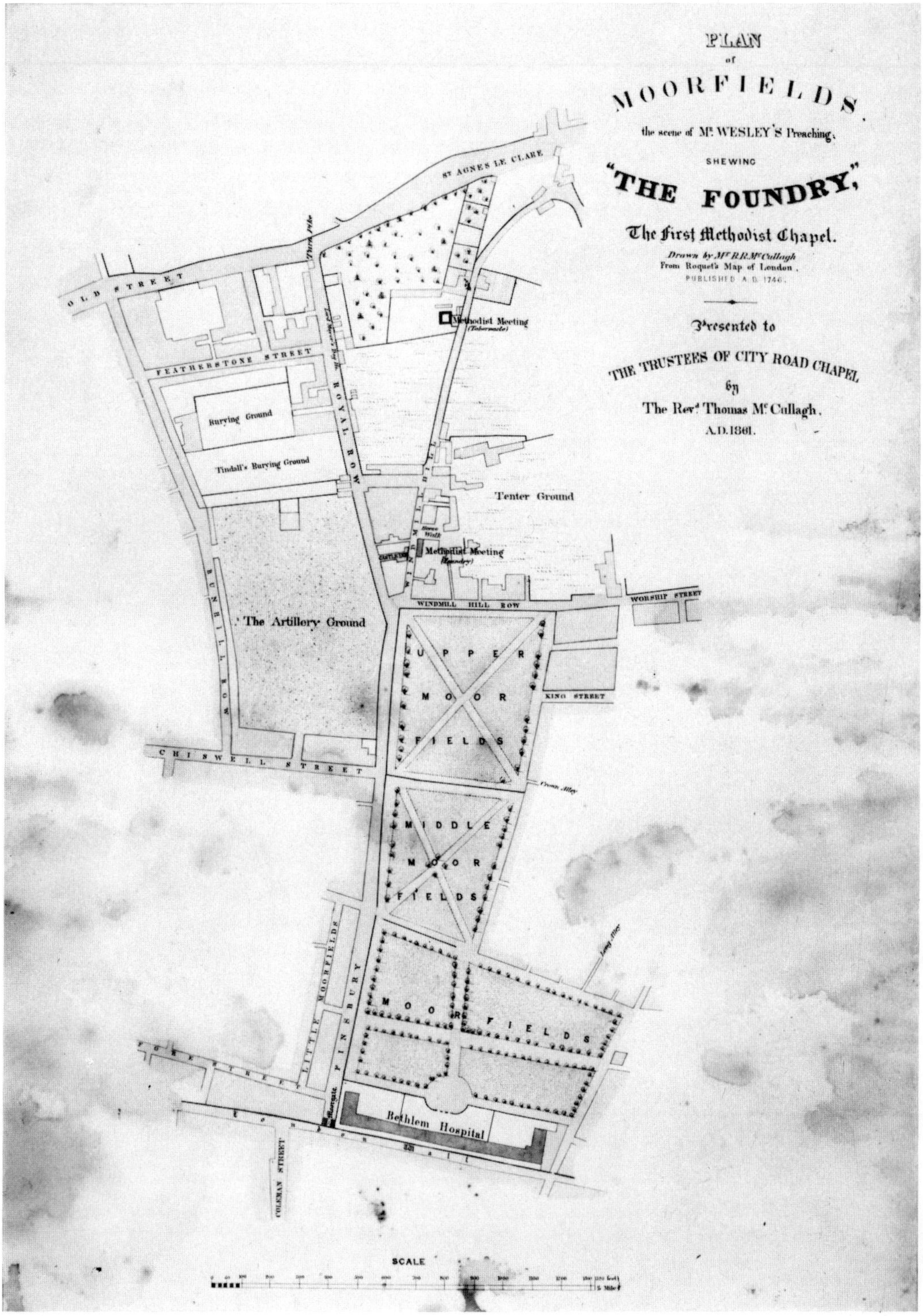

PLAN
of
MOORFIELDS.
the scene of Mr WESLEY'S Preaching,
SHEWING
"THE FOUNDRY,"
The First Methodist Chapel.
Drawn by Mr R R McCullagh
From Roque's Map of London.
PUBLISHED A.D. 1746.

Presented to
THE TRUSTEES OF CITY ROAD CHAPEL
by
The Revd Thomas McCullagh,
A.D. 1861.

ST AGNES LE CLARE

OLD STREET

Peerless Pool

FEATHERSTONE STREET

ROYAL ROW

Methodist Meeting
(Tabernacle)

Burying Ground

Tindall's Burying Ground

Tenter Ground

Methodist Meeting
(Foundry)

BUNHILL ROW

The Artillery Ground

WINDMILL HILL ROW

WORSHIP STREET

UPPER
MOOR
FIELDS

KING STREET

CHISWELL STREET

Crown Alley

MIDDLE
MOOR
FIELDS

LITTLE MOORFIELDS

FINSBURY

MOOR FIELDS

GRUB STREET

Bishopsgate

LONDON WALL

Bethlem Hospital

COLEMAN STREET

SCALE

1/8 Mile

During the winter of 1739, Charles took on the Bristol mission, particularly working among the Kingswood miners. Opposition grew. The clergy came out solidly against the Wesleys and Whitefield. A Dr Trapp finished a diatribe with the injunction: 'Go not after the impostors and seducers; but shun them as you would the plague.' The bitterness stemmed partly from the fact that the churches were half empty while the Gospel was being preached outside to the masses. There was also a snobbish element of dismay that well-educated, well-connected gentry like the Wesleys should indulge in such a rough-and-tumble. The Bishop of Armagh, meeting Charles at Clifton, said: 'I know your brother well. I could never credit all I heard respecting him and you.'

In the spring of 1740 John went back to Bristol to organize the school for poor children and classes of adults at Kingswood. There reports reached him that Thomas Maxfield had been preaching to the people at the Foundery. He immediately took horse to put a stop to what he regarded as presumption. The young man had not confined himself to expounding the scripture or reading the text of one of Wesley's sermons; he was preaching sermons of his own. But when, much agitated, Wesley told his mother, 'Thomas Maxfield has turned preacher', old Susanna surprised him by saying: 'Take care what you do with respect to that young man, for he is as surely called of God to preach as you are. Examine what have been the fruits of his preaching: and hear him also yourself.'

His mother was still the strongest individual influence in John's life. He took her advice and went to hear Maxfield preaching in the Foundery. Afterwards he declared, 'It is the Lord's doing. Let him do what seemeth good. What am I, that I should withstand God?' So

'The origin of Sunday Schools': an eighteenth-century engraving.

Maxfield was formally accepted as a lay preacher, and this was an historic decision. In the course of the next twelve months Wesley appointed twenty more, and was eventually to be at the head of a force of almost 700. He would never have been able to consolidate a nationwide religious movement without lay preachers to sustain the organization, and to replenish it spiritually. He did not foresee, or he took a calculated risk, that by employing laymen of slender education to preach the Gospel, some self-taught, many of them of the artisan class, he was goading the Establishment to fresh fury. A preacher, however poor, should speak and dress like a gentleman! One of the chief iniquities of John Wesley was that he was letting down his class.

From 1740 till 1760 meetings were repeatedly disrupted by mobs often organized, and nearly always protected, by local magistrates and clergy. Methodists' houses and belongings were destroyed, serious and sometimes fatal injuries inflicted, and preachers were regularly beaten up. One of the first manifestations of physical violence was in the autumn of 1740, when a mob of shouting men forced their way into the Foundery. The following year stones were flung at Wesley in Marylebone Fields. At Hoxton an ox was driven into his congregation – a favourite gambit of Methodist-baiters. In the long history of harassment and assault Wesley never showed fear. He often cowed and even converted his persecutors. He coolly gave them vigorous retort: he also showed compassion and pity.

In the early 1740s he began to range further afield. From the outset as an itinerant preacher he was well organized: but he had to contend with appalling roads. Daniel Defoe had recently written: 'The country

Kingswood School, Bristol, completed in 1740 for the education of poor children. The drawing is by one of the early headmasters, T. M'Greary.

indeed remains in the utmost distress for want of good roads.' Arthur Young, later in the century – when Wesley was still travelling – stated, 'In all England there are but four good roads; the rest it would be a Prostitution of Language to call Turnpikes.'

The system, if it could be so called, was that the King's Highways were farmed out to private companies, and these erected turnpike gates which provided income for a minimum of effort. It was said of Wesley that he paid more tolls than any man who ever bestrode beast. He usually hired horses, sometimes three in the course of a single journey. He rode from London to Oxford in one day, changing horses twice. The roads were nowhere amenable to speed, being full of pot holes, deep rutted and undrained, so he took advantage of the slow progress – and greatly added to the hazards – by reading and even composing as he rode, letting the reins fall on the horse's neck. The fairly frequent tumbles broke no bones, and the bruises were always treated by an application of warm treacle on brown paper. Between 1738 and 1790 he journeyed more than a quarter of a million miles by road, in his later years using a carriage.

After visits to South Wales in 1741 and 1742 he made his first assault on the north of England. A letter from the stonemason John Nelson, who had gathered a flock of ardent converts at Birstall, begged Wesley as his father in Christ to advise him how to continue his work. Not least of Nelson's anxieties was the disapproval he encountered, because of his uncouth, downright language, from Benjamin Ingham,

The length and breadth of the kingdom were covered many times by John Wesley in the course of his fifty years of itinerancy, during which he is estimated to have marked up 250,000 miles, mainly on horseback. Two contemporary views of the country's turnpikes, lanes and staging-posts (*below and opposite*), as Wesley might have known them. *Opposite*, in a letter to John Hervey, 25 October 1739, Wesley for the first time expresses his view that the whole world was his parish.

"But you'd have me preach it in a Parish." What Parish, my Brother? I have none at all. Nor I believe ever shall. Must I therefore bury my Talent in the Earth? Then am I a wicked, unprofitable Servant.

The Constitution of the Apostolical Church is as much for our preaching Every where, as the Example of the Apostles. The travels of Timothy are recorded in ye Acts. Nor do I believe either He or Titus, or any Xtian Minister was confined to any one Place, till ye Love of Xtians waxed cold.

But indeed, I could not serve (as they term it) a Cure now. I have tried, & know it is Impracticable, to observe the Laws of ye English Church, in any Parish in England. I observed them in my Parish of Savannah, till I was obliged to fly for my Life. Mr Stonehouse is now persecuted on every side, for observing ym: And the Good Bishop, instead of defending his Presbyter, is at the Head of his Persecutors.

Set the matter in another Light, & it comes to a short Issue. I every where see God's people perishing for lack of Knowledge. I have power (thro' God) to save their Souls from Death. Shall I use it, or shall I let ym perish — because they are not of my Parish?

The city of Newcastle, for which John Wesley had a special fondness. Even violence was less vicious there: 'The very mob . . . in the height of their violence,' he wrote, 'have commonly some humanity left.'

Wesley's companion in Georgia, now conducting a revival of his own in the West Riding. Wesley gave his blessing and preached to the Birstall people. John Nelson's conduct of affairs put a stop to any misgivings he had about lay preachers.

Then, accompanied by his servant John Taylor, he left Birstall on May 27 and arrived in Newcastle, a hundred-mile trek, the following day. He was charmed by pre-industrial revolution Newcastle: 'If I did not believe there was another world, I should spend all my summers here, as I know no place in Great Britain comparable to it for pleasantness.' No doubt these thoughts came to him in the 'better parts' of the city. He was soon horrified by the street scenes in the poorer parts: 'So much drunkenness, cursing, and swearing (even from the mouths of little children), do I never remember to have seen and heard before, in so small a compass of time.'

From this unpropitious start there followed one of the greatest achievements of his long preaching career, which must be told in his own eloquent words:

'I walked down to Sandgate, the poorest and most contemptible part of the town; and, standing at the end of the street with John Taylor, began to sing the Hundredth Psalm. Three or four people came out to see what was the matter, who soon increased to four or five hundred. I suppose there might be twelve or fifteen hundred, before I had done preaching; . . .

'Observing the people . . . to stand gaping and staring at me, with
the most profound astonishment, I told them, "If you desire to know
who I am, my name is John Wesley. At five this evening, with God's
help, I design to preach here again."

'At five, the hill on which I designed to preach was covered from
the top to the bottom. I never saw so large a number of people together,
either in Moorfields or at Kennington Common. I knew it was not
possible for the one half to hear . . . and I stood so as to have them all in
view as they were ranged on the side of the hill. The Word of God
which I set before them was, "I will heal their backsliding, I will love
them freely." After preaching, the poor people were ready to tread me
under foot, out of pure love and kindness. It was some time before I
could possibly get out of the press. I then went back another way than I
came, but several were got to our inn before me; by whom I was
vehemently importuned to stay with them, at least a few days. . . . But I
could not consent, having given my word to be at Birstall, with God's
leave, on Tuesday night.'

Following that amazing start, Newcastle became the most potent
centre of Methodism in the north. Charles went there to continue his
brother's work. Then, later in the year, John went back for six weeks.
He bought a site for a meeting house and initiated the building of a
home for orphans with a capacity for forty children. His Sunday
school was soon teaching 1,000 pupils a week – at a time when

John Wesley preaching on his father's tombstone at Epworth, 6 June 1742, to 'a vast multitude gathered from all parts'. Remembering his father's disappointing life he wrote in his journal, 'O let none think his labour of love is lost because the fruit does not immediately appear.'

education for the poor was unknown. Miners who came to hear him preach in the evening would spend the night sleeping on hard benches in order to hear him again the following morning.

After his first Newcastle visit Wesley, in some trepidation but with a sense of duty, rode to Epworth on a Saturday: 'I went to an inn in the middle of the town, not knowing whether there were any left in it now who would be ashamed of my acquaintance.' The curate in charge, the Rev. John Romley, rejected John's offer to preach and himself delivered a sermon against religious enthusiasm in general and against Methodism in particular. As the congregation left they found John Taylor in the churchyard with the message that 'Mr Wesley, not being permitted to preach in the church, designs to preach here at six o'clock'.

A great crowd, certainly the largest congregation Epworth had ever seen, listened to John Wesley as he stood on his father's tombstone. For six days running he preached to enthusiastic multitudes, some of whom were stricken with frenzy and thrown to the ground. He also spent a day preaching at Wroote, where he had served briefly as curate, and where his brother-in-law John Whitelamb was now minister.

Methodists had already been persecuted in the district. Wesley went to visit a Justice of the Peace to whom a waggon-load of Methodists had been driven by hostile mobs. He was told that it was because they pretended to be better than other people and prayed from morning till night. One accuser added that they had converted his wife: 'Till she went among them, she had such a tongue. And now she is as quiet as a lamb.'

'Carry them back,' said the Justice, more liberal than most of his kind. 'Let them convert all the scolds in town.' Very soon Wesley's followers in all parts of the country were being dragged before magistrates on various charges; this and widespread physical persecution were to continue for much of his lifetime. At Epworth nothing mollified the hostility of the Rev. John Romley. On Wesley's next visit he sent word: 'Pray tell Mr Wesley I shall not give him the sacrament, for he is not fit.' There was no doubt that the established Church initiated much of the violence. Yet the Wesleys never wavered in their loyalty to the Church until nearly the end of John's active life, when schism became inevitable.

By the end of 1742 the movement and Wesley's fame had spread. The Foundery, Bristol and Kingswood had expanded. New societies had started in Leicester, Warwickshire, Gloucester and Somerset. Strong in support of Methodism, proud and shrewd Susanna Wesley died in that year at the Foundery, and was buried in Bunhill Fields, John conducting the service with an 'almost innumerable company of

The burial of Susanna Wesley, 1742, attended by 'one of the most solemn assemblies I ever saw, or expect to see on this side eternity'. *Below*, John Wesley visiting his mother's grave, 1779.

Susanna Wesley, the matriarch of Methodism, towards the end of her life. At her deathbed she said: 'Children, as soon as I am released, sing a psalm of praise to God.'

people being gathered there'. She had shared quarters at the Foundery with John. It was the nearest to a home that he was to know. It was now accepted that he and Charles were to be itinerant evangelists, never duplicating the effort by travelling together, though they frequently followed one another over the same territory. The lay preachers worked from fixed points. From the Foundery John – it was he who undertook all the organizing – created a nationwide pattern. People were grouped in 'classes', each with a leader. A penny a week was collected from each member, with the richer members making up the shortfall, if necessary. Those who acted unworthily were dismissed. There was no admission without some definite proof of religious 'intentions'. Membership inevitably caused a slight rise in social status and an image of exclusiveness. So the network of Wesleyan organization provided an opportunity for violence which was overtly or secretly encouraged by the Establishment.

One of the most curious affrays was in 1743 at Wednesbury, Staffordshire, where John, followed by Charles, had established a flourishing society. Unfortunately a subsequent preacher denounced the local clergy, with the result that the local vicar preached against Methodism 'with great bitterness of voice and manner'.

Then mob violence started. An eyewitness, James Jones, described it as follows: 'The mob . . . assaulted, one after another, all the houses of those who were called Methodists. They first broke all their windows. Then they made their way in; and all the tables, chairs, chests of drawers, with whatever was not easily removable, they dashed in pieces. . . . What they could not well break, as feather-beds, they cut in pieces and strewed about the room. William Sitch's wife was lying in; but that was all one; they pulled away her bed too, and cut it in pieces.'

Some of the gentry, who supported such violence, threatened to dismiss miners who did not take part in the riot. They tried to force the persecuted to sign declarations that they would never invite or entertain a Methodist minister. The disorders lasted six June days. By the time Wesley arrived they had subsided. He returned again in October and preached at midday in the centre of the town, 'to a far larger congregation then was expected . . . and no creature offered to molest us.' The first reaction of Wednesbury was one of awe at such a bold stance in their midst.

Trouble began at five o'clock in the afternoon, when the house where Wesley was staying was beset by a mob crying: 'Bring out the Minister; we will have the Minister.' Wesley invited the leader of the riot to come in. 'After a few sentences interchanged between us, the lion was become a lamb. I desired him to go and bring one or two more

Methodism and the mob: the violence at Wednesbury, like that at many other anti-Methodist riots, was actively supported by the local Church and squirearchy.

of the most angry of his companions. He brought in two who were ready to swallow the ground with rage; but in two minutes they were as calm as he. I then bade them make way, that I might go out among the people.'

It was characteristic of the amazing coolness and courage he showed at all times that John Wesley climbed on a chair in the midst of them and cried: 'What do you want with me?' They shouted that they wanted him to go with them to the Justice. 'That I will, with all my heart,' Wesley said. 'Shall we go to the Justice tonight, or in the morning?'

They insisted that it should be that night. Several hundred of them set out, with darkness coming on and in heavy rain, to walk two miles to Bentley Hall, but the magistrate refused to appear, sending a message that he had gone to bed and advising everyone to do the same. The crowd then took Wesley on to a magistrate at Walsall. To their dismay he had also gone to bed early, or so he chose to maintain.

Some fifty men in the crowd now formed an escort to take Wesley back to Wednesbury, but word had got round that he was in Walsall, and a local mob determined to capture him. They poured in like a flood, and bore down all before them. Wesley's escort was 'weary as well as outnumbered: so that in a short time many were being knocked down, the rest ran away.' Wesley was left to his Walsall captors. We have his own account of what followed:

'To attempt speaking was vain; for the noise on every side was like the roaring of the sea. So they dragged me along till we came to the town; where seeing the door of a large house open, I attempted to go in; but a man, catching me by the hair, pulled me back into the middle of the mob. They made no more stop till they had carried me through the main street, from one end of the town to the other. I continued speaking all the time to those within hearing, feeling no pain or weariness. At the west end of the town, seeing a door half open, I made toward it, and would have gone in; but a gentleman in the shop would not suffer me, saying, they would pull the house down to the ground. However, I stood at the door, and asked, "Are you willing to hear me speak?" Many cried out, "No, no! knock his brains out; down with him; kill him at once." Others said, "Nay, but we will hear him first." I began asking, "What evil have I done? Which of you all have I wronged in word or deed?" and continued speaking for about a quarter of an hour, till my voice suddenly failed; then the floods began to lift up their voice again; many crying out, "Bring him away! bring him away!"

'In the meantime my strength and my voice returned, and I broke out aloud into prayer. And now the man who just before headed the mob, turned, and said, "Sir, I will spend my life for you: follow me, and not one soul here shall touch a hair of your head." Two or three of his fellows confirmed his words, and got close to me immediately. At the same time, the gentleman in the shop cried out, "For shame, for shame! Let him go." An honest butcher, who was a little farther off, said it was a shame they should do thus; and pulled back four or five, one after another, who were running on the most fiercely. The people then, as if it had been by common consent, fell back to the right and left; while those three or four men took me between them, and carried me through them all. But on the bridge the mob rallied again; we therefore went on one side, over the mill dam, and thence through the meadows; till, a little before ten, God brought me safe to Wednesbury; having lost only one flap of my waistcoat, and a little skin from one of my hands.'

He noted afterwards that he had thought they would throw him in the river, and that 'it would spoil the papers that were in my pocket. . . . I did not doubt but that I should swim across, having but a thin coat and a light pair of boots.' He had indeed been lightly clad for this ordeal on a wet October night. The next day he rode through the town unmolested on his way to Nottingham. On the way he read the following notice:

'Whereas, we, His Majesty's Justices of the Peace for the said County of Stafford, having received information that several disorderly persons, styling themselves Methodist Preachers, go about raising routs and riots, to the great damage of His Majesty's liege people, and against the peace of our Sovereign Lord the King:

'These are, in His Majesty's name, to command you and every one of you, within your respective districts, to make diligent search after the said Methodist Preachers, and to bring him or them before some of us His said Majesty's Justices of the Peace, to be examined concerning their unlawful doings.'

It had been signed by the two magistrates who had refused to get out of bed. At Nottingham his brother Charles met him, and reported that his clothes were torn and he was covered with scars and scratches. He urged Charles to go on to Wednesbury and Walsall to stiffen the morale of the faithful.

Within twenty-four hours he was involved in another adventure, caused not by man but nature. He was committed to preach at Grimsby, 'but at Ferry we were at a full stop, the boatmen telling us we could not pass the Trent; it was as much as our lives were worth to put from shore before the storm abated. We waited an hour; but, being afraid it would do much hurt, if I should disappoint the congregation at Grimsby, I asked the men if they did not think it possible to get to the other shore; they said, they could not tell; but if we would venture our lives, they would venture theirs. So we put off, having six men, two women, and three horses, in the boat. Many stood looking after us on the riverside, in the middle of which we were, when, in an instant, the

John Wesley preaching at Nottingham to segregated audiences.

Ferry, at the Trent near Epworth, where John Wesley barely escaped drowning on his way to Grimsby, October 1743.

side of the boat was under water, and the horses and men rolling one over another. We expected the boat to sink every moment; but I did not doubt of being able to swim ashore. . . . And soon after, our horses leaping overboard, lightened the boat, and we all came unhurt to land.

'They wondered what was the matter I did not rise, and I wondered too, till I found that a large iron crow was . . . run through the string of my boot, which pinned me down so that, if the boat had sunk, I should have been safe enough from swimming any further.'

Wesley's tight schedules and insistence on punctuality certainly required an iron constitution.

Besides becoming the targets for so much physical violence, John and Charles were subjected to every kind of vilification by rumour, vicious gossip and false report. Dissenters and Catholics were hated minorities, and Wesley was at various times accused of belonging to both. This was particularly hard to bear as he remained steadfastly loyal to the Church of England until nearly the end of his time. Stories were current that he had been arrested for unlawfully selling gin, that he had committed suicide, that he was an impostor, the real Wesley being long since dead. The most dangerous was the imputation that the Wesleys were Jacobites – the '45 was to come – and that Methodism was an underground subversive movement. Charles inadvertently added to this suspicion when he prayed to God 'to bring home his banished'; for him a figure of speech, to his enemies a confirmation that he looked to the Prince over the Water. The most fantastic rumour had it that John Wesley had been seen in the company of the Pretender in France. A novel form of persecution was inflicted in Cornwall when John arrived in the summer of 1743. He was preaching in the street when a man accosted him: 'Sir, I have a warrant from Dr Borlase, and you must go with me.' This Dr Borlase, a magistrate, had the notion of pressing Wesley into military service abroad – several lay preachers had been singled out by press-gangs. When he found Wesley to be an educated and articulate man and a gentleman to boot, Borlase immediately ordered Wesley's release. But before the day was out Wesley, preaching in the street, was interrupted by a party of horsemen, one of whom cried: 'Seize him! Seize him! Seize the preacher for His Majesty's service.' The speaker jumped down from his horse and clutched Wesley by his gown, saying: 'I take you to serve His Majesty', and marched him away. Wesley simply talked his way out of this arrest and concluded: 'He then called for his horse, and another for me, and rode back to the place whence he took me.'

In Cornwall there were several more ugly confrontations, and a meeting house was pulled down by the mob. Yet Wesley recorded at

Bickman's map of Cornwall (1750), where Wesley travelled extensively on his preaching tours, suffered some violence, and had some of his greatest successes.

John Wesley preaching in the natural amphitheatre near Gwennap, Cornwall.

the end, 'I concluded my preaching here. We reached Gwennap . . . and found the plain covered from end to end. It was supposed there were 10,000 people.' Gwennap Pit, a natural amphitheatre near Redruth still exists and holds a congregation of 2,000, usually filled at Whitsuntide.

In 1744 Wesley called his first Conference. It consisted of six Anglican clergymen and four lay preachers. He had divided Methodism into Societies, Classes, Bands and Select Societies. The Conference was intended as the ruling body. The agenda of the first Conference included what and how to teach; and how to regulate doctrine, discipline and practice. When it was over they all attended Holy Communion, emphasizing their membership of the Church of England which in every part of the country was closing its doors to them. At that period no Methodist meetings were allowed by Wesley to be held at the times of Anglican services.

Wesley's advice to preachers was crisp and professional:

'Endeavour to speak in public just as you do in common conversation.

'Labour to avoid the odious custom of coughing and spitting while you are speaking. And if at some times you cannot wholly avoid it, yet take care you do not stop in the middle of a sentence, but only at such times as will least interrupt the sense of what you are delivering.

'To drawl is worse than to hurry.

'The good and honourable actions of men should be described with a full and lofty accent; wicked and infamous actions, with a strong and earnest voice, and such a tone as expresses horror and detestation.

'The mouth must never be turned awry; neither must you bite or lick your lips, or shrug your shoulders, or lean upon your elbow; all which give just offence to the spectators.

'Never clap your hands, nor thump the pulpit.

'Your hands are not to be in perpetual motion: this the ancients called the babbling of the hands.

'And when, by such assistances as these, you have acquired a good habit of speaking, you will no more need any tedious reflections upon this art, but will speak as easily as gracefully.'

In addition to these precepts, Wesley urged his itinerant preachers to remain single. God's work put an almost intolerable burden on marriage – except in special cases which, as we shall see, were to include himself.

That he was attractive to women there is no doubt, and he enjoyed their company. In spite of the wear and tear of preaching about fourteen times every week, and riding in all weathers fifteen to twenty miles a day, he kept himself presentable. He always wore plain, neat, black clothes. His jackets had upright collars, from which flowed the white bands of the Anglican clergyman of the period. He never wore silk or velvet. For preaching in the open air he put on a black flowing cassock. He wore his own hair, long. It was admired by both his friends and enemies. During the Wednesbury rioting, he recorded in his journal, an assailant 'came rushing through the press, and raising his arm to strike, on a sudden let it drop, and only stroked my head, saying "What soft hair he has."' In his forties he was still lean, muscular and graceful. He suffered little sickness, but when he was stricken he always attracted female nursing, as he did with Miss Sophy and as he was to do again.

In 1746 he founded a dispensary for the poor in London. He also set up a galvanic apparatus for treating people by electricity. Many of his own remedies were homely. For hoarseness he recommended: 'Rub the soles of the feet before the fire with garlic and lard well beaten together.' For baldness, 'Rub your scalp with honey and onions, and electrify daily.'

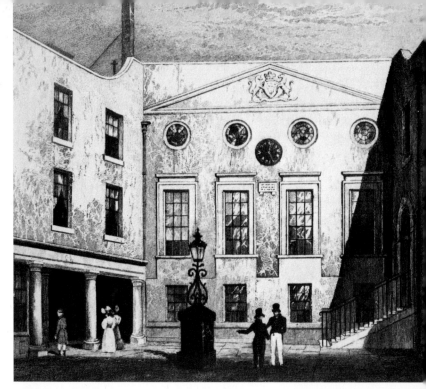

Wesley had a pragmatic though unsophisticated interest in medicine, setting up dispensaries and trying out the latest techniques, such as an electrification machine (*below*). He wrote a do-it-yourself handbook of medicine (*below right*), and ordered his medical supplies from the reputable Apothecaries' Hall (*right*).

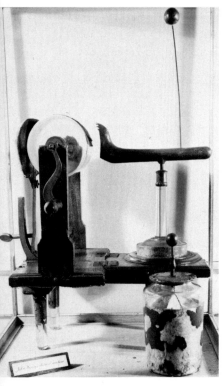

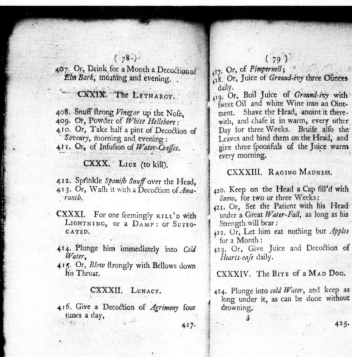

(78)

407. Or, Drink for a Month a Decoction of *Elm Bark*, morning and evening.

CXXIX. The LETHARGY.

408. Snuff strong *Vinegar* up the Nose,
409. Or, Powder of *White Hellebore* :
410. Or, Take half a pint of Decoction of *Savoury*, morning and evening :
411. Or, of Infusion of *Water-Cresses*.

CXXX. LICE (to kill).

412. Sprinkle *Spanish Snuff* over the Head,
413. Or, Wash it with a Decoction of *Amaranth*.

CXXXI. For one seemingly KILL'D with LIGHTNING, or a DAMP: or SUFFOCATED.

414. Plunge him immediately into *Cold Water*,
415. Or, Blow strongly with Bellows down his Throat.

CXXXII. LUNACY.

416. Give a Decoction of *Agrimony* four times a day,

417.

(79)

417. Or, of *Pimpernell* ;
418. Or, Juice of *Ground-ivy* three Ounces daily.
419. Or, Boil Juice of *Ground-ivy* with sweet Oil and white Wine into an Ointment. Shave the Head, anoint it therewith, and chafe it in warm, every other Day for three Weeks. Bruise also the Leaves and bind them on the Head, and give three spoonfuls of the Juice warm every morning.

CXXXIII. RAGING MADNESS.

420. Keep on the Head a Cap fill'd with *Snow*, for two or three Weeks:
421. Or, Set the Patient with his Head under a Great *Water-Fall*, as long as his Strength will bear :
422. Or, Let him eat nothing but *Apples* for a Month :
423. Or, Give Juice and Decoction of *Hearts-ease* daily.

CXXXIV. The BITE of a MAD DOG.

424. Plunge into *cold Water*, and keep as long under it, as can be done without drowning.

3

425.

In August 1748 John Wesley, now aged forty-five, fell ill while at Newcastle, and Grace Murray, a widow, nursed him. This Grace had been converted ten years before, and had proved herself an exceptional worker, both in London and Newcastle, where she was appointed to take charge of the orphan house. Wesley had long been aware of her qualities, and had chosen her as one of the select group accompanying him on his field-preaching tours. Her particular role was to oversee the female classes, and it was said that her services as a female itinerant were popular and successful. At Newcastle she also took on duties as a nurse for the preachers – and it was said that preachers in that area were more frequently sick than elsewhere, for she was an attractive woman. Two years earlier, one of her patients had been John Bennet, a Bolton preacher of good family who lay twenty-six weeks in the orphan house with a fever. He fell in love and made proposals, but she was a vacillating creature who could not bring herself to give the young man a direct answer.

John Wesley had observed her with approval over a number of years, though the idea of marriage itself may not have arisen till this moment of maximum susceptibility. In his private diary he revealed his thoughts of marriage and his assessment of her character – strange thoughts for a lover, perhaps: 'I now clearly perceive, that my Marriage would bring little Expense if I married one I maintain now, who would afterwards desire nothing more than she had before. And would cheerfully consent, that our children (if any) should be wholly brought up at Kingswood. . . . I am persuaded she is in every Capacity an Help meet for me. First, as a Housekeeper. Then, as a nurse, she is indefatigably patient, and inexpressibly tender. She is quick, cleanly, skilful, and understands my Constitution better than most Physicians.'

He then tells us how he, tentatively, proposed to her and she, tentatively, replied: 'I was taken ill at Newcastle. Grace Murray attended me continually. I observ'd her more narrowly than ever before, both as to her temper, sense and behaviour. I esteem'd and lov'd her more and more. And when I was a little recover'd, I told her, sliding into it I know not how: "If I ever marry, I think you will be the Person." After some time, I spoke to her more directly. She seem'd utterly amazed, and said: "This is too great a Blessing for me: I can't tell how to believe it. This is all I could have wished for under heaven, if I had dar'd to wish for it."'

After John's proposal, if one could call it that, he made ready to ride south, first telling Grace that 'he was convinced God had called her to be his fellow labourer in the Gospel.' He also suggested he should take her with him to Ireland in the following spring. Grace was unwilling to think that far ahead. She pleaded with him to let her travel with him there and then, and he agreed.

The Newcastle orphan house, supervised by Grace Murray.

A southeast prospect of Leeds, scene of a sad reconciliation when John Wesley encountered his brother after Grace Murray's wedding to Bennet.

Opposite, Charles Wesley and his wife Sarah, née Gwynne. *Below*, the house in Charles Street, Bristol, which was Charles Wesley's home for twenty years.

Her company did not prevent him from reading on horseback: 'In riding to Leeds I read Dr Hodge's *Account of the Plague in London*.' They were accompanied by Mockford, a lay preacher, and completed a preaching tour of Yorkshire, lodging at the home of John Bennet at Chinley. Grace must have known about this arrangement and apparently found it no embarrassment, though she had never actually turned down Bennet. Wesley, all unaware of this situation, asked Bennet to 'take good care of Mrs Murray', and went on to London.

Grace then accompanied Bennet on a preaching tour of Derbyshire, during which he begged her to become his wife. She said: 'If Mr Wesley will give his consent, I will yield.' They then both wrote letters to Wesley. Bennet asked permission to marry her; Grace wrote that she believed God intended her for John Bennet. Amazed, Wesley sent 'a mild answer to both, supposing they were already married'.

Grace then returned to Newcastle and started an affectionate but noncommittal correspondence with both Wesley and Bennet. The next astonishing turn was that she announced to Bennet that she was going with Wesley to Ireland. If Bennet loved her he should meet her in Sheffield on her way south or she could not answer for the consequences. The unfortunate Bennet missed her, and she went on

and met Wesley at Bristol. Thence they travelled into Wales where, on 3 April 1749, John officiated at the wedding of Charles Wesley to Sarah Gwynne at Garth, Breconshire. The celibacy of field-preachers was no longer a *sine qua non*, and in any case Charles was soon to give up itinerancy. His bride was the daughter of a wealthy landowner and magistrate who, from being an opponent, had become a patron of Methodism.

Wesley then went on to Ireland with Grace and a company of preachers, remaining there from April 15 till July 20. Of Grace's conduct there he wrote, 'I saw the work of God prosper in her hands. . . . She lightened my Burden more than can be exprest. She examin'd all the Women in the smaller Societies and the Believers in every place. . . . Meantime she was to me both a Servant and Friend as well as a Fellow-labourer in the Gospel. She provided everything I wanted.'

Before leaving Dublin they had entered upon a somewhat nebulous provisional contract of marriage, *De praesenti*. But on returning to Bristol Grace resumed contact with Bennet, who wrote to say that if John married Grace it would 'destroy all the work of God that was in their hands', and that all Methodists were against the match. Wesley and Grace then travelled to Epworth to meet Bennet, where Wesley was persuaded that it would be better if she married Bennet. However, the situation remained unresolved, since Grace accompanied Wesley to Newcastle, leaving Bennet at Epworth. At Newcastle she announced that she was 'determined, by conscience as well as by inclination, to live and die' with Wesley. Accepting this, he wrote a letter to Bennet, which was never received, and sent a copy to his brother Charles – the brothers had agreed that neither should marry without the consent of the other. He and Grace then renewed the Dublin contract before witnesses, and it was duly attested at Allandale, after which Wesley rode off to Whitehaven. His programme of travelling and preaching went on regardless, as the journal shows.

Charles's reaction to his brother's wedding was extraordinarily violent. He immediately travelled post-haste to Whitehaven, where he told John, as the latter recorded in his journal, that 'the thought of my *marrying* at all, but especially of my marrying a Servant, and one so low-born, appear'd above measure shocking to him. Thence he infer'd that it would break up all our Societies, and put a stop to the whole work of God.'

Wesley was unimpressed by such arguments, but the next day, without saying a word to John, Charles rode to the village where Grace was staying with friends. 'Grace Murray!' he burst out, 'You have broken my heart,' and fainted. Recovering, the author of 'Gentle Jesus, Meek and Mild' showered Grace with reproaches, urged her to give up all idea of marriage to his brother, who was obviously out of his mind, and finally induced her to believe she was obliged to marry John Bennet. Then he rode back to Newcastle to tackle the weary Bennet, who now refused to have her back as his future wife. But Charles Wesley would not take no for an answer. He rode back and fetched Grace on the pillion of his horse. He then simply forced a reconciliation.

John Wesley, therefore, returned from Whitehaven to be told, 'Mr Charles left us two hours since, and carried Sister Murray behind him.' Wesley's self-control did not waver, but the next day was devoted to praying, fasting and self-examination 'touching what was so confidently laid to my charge, viz., inordinate affection'. But how, he asked himself, could he condemn as 'inordinate affection' a feeling which increased his appetite for God's work, made him 'more sensible of the Power and Presence of God', and afforded him not the smallest jealousy 'even of J.B., nor a minute's resentment towards those who tore her from me'? Returning to Whitehaven the next day he wrote, 'I need add no more, than that if I had had more Regard for her I loved than for the Work of God, I should now have gone straight on to Newcastle, and not back to Whitehaven.' Bennet and Grace were married a few days later.

Wesley's sorrow was expressed in a letter he wrote to the lay preacher John Bigg a few days after the wedding: 'For ten years God has been preparing a fellow labourer for me, by a wonderful train of providence. Last year I was convinced of it; therefore I delayed not, but, as I thought, made all sure beyond a danger of disappointment. But we were soon afterwards torn asunder by a whirlwind. . . . The whole world fought against me; but above all, my own familiar friend.'

John Wesley was one of the most forgiving of men, but in this case there was much to forgive. Nevertheless, a reconciliation took place between the two brothers shortly afterwards, thanks largely to the compassionate services of Whitefield, who was then at Leeds. Wesley recorded the event in his journal:

'One came in from Newcastle, and told us, "They were married on Tuesday." My brother came an hour after. I felt no anger, yet I did not desire to see him. But Mr Whitefield constrained me. After a few words had passed, he [Whitefield] accosted me with "I renounce all intercourse with you, but what I would have with an heathen man or a publican." I felt little emotion. It was only adding a cup of water to a drowning man, yet I calmly accepted his renunciation and acquiesced therein. Poor Mr Whitefield and John Nelson burst into tears. They prayed, cried and entreated, till the storm passed away. We could not speak, but only fell on each other's neck.

'John Bennet then came in. Neither of us could speak, but we kissed each other and wept. Soon after I talked with my brother alone. He seemed utterly amazed. He clearly saw I was not what he thought, and now blamed her only; which confirmed me in believing my presage was true, and I should see her face no more.'

John Wesley's real marriage was to his work. He listened, however, to friends who suggested that he should find a middle-aged lady who was not mixed up with the organization of Methodism. Such a marriage would reassure his followers and strengthen public confidence in his work. In February 1751 he was telling his men that marriage was a hindrance: 'I met the single men, and showed them on how many counts it was good for those who had received that gift from God to remain "single for the kingdom of heaven's sake"; unless where a particular case might be an exception to the general rule.'

He himself was the exception. In the same month he noted in his journal, 'I was clearly convinced that I ought to marry. For many years I remained single, because I believed I could be more useful in a single than in a married state. And I praise God, who enabled me so to do. I now as fully believed that in my present circumstances I might be more useful in a married state.'

For the third time it was kindly nursing that attracted his affection. This time for a wealthy forty-one-year-old widow, Mrs Molly Vazeille. This lady had become a friend of Charles and his wife, and of

Mary
wife of
John Wesley

several of the Wesleys' London friends. Her husband had been Anthony Noah Vazeille, a Huguenot merchant with a house in Threadneedle Street and a country place at Wandsworth. She herself was interested in Methodism. She had several children, was an excellent mother and had considerable social charm. Little is known about their courtship except for one significant episode which may have begun it. On 10 February 1751 Wesley had a heavy fall on the frozen road in the middle of London Bridge. He was carried by chair to Mrs Vazeille's house in Threadneedle Street, and was nursed by her. His journal makes this sound unromantic to a degree: 'I spent the remainder of the week, partly in prayer, reading and conversation, partly in writing an *Hebrew Grammar*, and *Lessons for Children*.' When Charles was informed of their engagement he was 'thunderstruck. I groaned all day, and several following ones, I could eat no pleasant food, nor preach, nor rest, either by night or by day.' Nevertheless, on February 18 the *Gentleman's Magazine* announced: 'Rev. Mr John Wesley, Methodist Preacher, to a Merchant's widow, with a jointure of £300 per annum.' The *London Magazine* also carried an announcement describing her as 'a widow lady of large fortune'. Nothing is known of the actual ceremony. No close friends were present, and Charles, to his chagrin, was not told about it till afterwards.

Both the Wesleys were almost penniless, though there was an increasing income from their publications. Yet each made a point of not touching his wife's fortune. John insisted on his bride's capital being secured on herself and her children.

Commemorative teapots recall the Methodist alternative to hard liquor: *above*, a picture of John Wesley encircled by a chain of his field-preachers; *below*, a teapot specially made and donated by Josiah Wedgwood.

John Wesley was determined that marriage should not interfere with God's work. He stated firmly, 'I cannot understand how a Methodist preacher can answer it to God to preach one sermon or travel one day less than in a single state.'

This was applied somewhat ruthlessly. He still had no home of his own, and Mrs Wesley found herself on the road facing foul weather and occasional outbursts of violence and stoning. She was constantly in the public eye, for her husband was now a nationwide celebrity. At first she tried to live up to his standards of endurance, but John, humane though he was, recognized her as a burden to him: 'In my Journey into the North, all my patience was put to the proof again and again; and all my endeavours to please, yet without success. In my present journey [alone] I leap as broke from chains. I am content with whatever entertainment I meet with, and my companions are always in good humour "because they are with me". This must be the spirit of all who take journeys with me. . . . To hear persons at my ear fretting and murmuring at every thing is like tearing the flesh off my bones.'

It was indeed a very bad match, as Charles had feared. Mrs Wesley's temperament and disposition began to change soon after marriage. She became hysterically jealous. Wesley's correspondence with female Methodists was often affectionate, and this provided Mrs Wesley with ammunition. She not only went through his correspondence, but handed items over to his Calvinist enemies in order that he should be discredited by their publication.

She found it impossible to respond to his suggestion, expressed in a letter, that she should 'leave me to be governed by God and by my conscience. Then I shall govern you with gentle sway and show you that I do indeed love you even as Christ the Church.' She was far from acting so submissively. In fact she seems to have been a regular termagant. We have an eyewitness account of an appalling scene between them, given by John Hampson who was not predisposed in Wesley's favour:

'Once I was on the point of committing murder. Once, when I was in the North of Ireland, I went into a room and found Mrs Wesley foaming with fury. Her husband was on the floor, where she had been trailing him by the hair of his head; and she was still holding in her hand venerable locks which she had plucked up by the roots. I felt as though I could have knocked the soul out of her.'

She deserted him on several occasions. In 1771 he wrote in his journal, 'For what cause I know not to this day [she] set out for Newcastle, purposing "never to return". *Non eam reliqui; non dimisi; non revocabo.* [I have not left her; I have not sent her away; I will not recall her.].' The unhappy woman died in 1781: 'I came to London, and was informed that my wife died on Monday. This evening she was buried, though I was not informed of it till a day or two later.'

The unsatisfactory love affairs of John Wesley must not be allowed to obscure the real stature of the man and his achievement. He had a profound effect on the British Isles in the eighteenth century, and he founded a worldwide religious society. In this short work it is impossible to follow in detail the year-by-year ardours and triumphs of his forty years of travel. They were repetitious in themselves. He never neglected the vineyards he had started. From 1760 onwards, Methodism advanced and consolidated throughout the country and America. Wesley's amazing itinerant activities continued well into his old age. He made one concession in using a carriage donated by friends. His very mobility prevented him from having many close friends, and his rooms at the Foundery, and later at the Chapel, were his only home.

With his travelling went a prodigious amount of writing. Like his reading, he continued it wherever he happened to be. He wrote 230 original works, besides the letters, journals and private diary. The official bibliography credits him with 417 items, but this last includes edited and abridged works, and some translations. By the time he was middle-aged he knew German, French, Spanish, Italian, Greek, Latin and Hebrew. He was a good conversationalist, though his restlessness irked Dr Johnson: 'John Wesley's conversation is good, but he is never at leisure. He is always obliged to go at a certain hour. This

Opposite, Romney's portrait of Wesley in old age. *Left*, relics of his travelling days (writing desk, carriage lamp and spurs), which continued well into his eighties.

Heptonstall Chapel, one of the first to be built by the Methodist movement. John Wesley laid the foundation stone in 1764.

is very disagreeable to a man who loves to fold his legs and have out his talk, as I do.'

Johnson also admired Wesley's preaching, as Boswell reported: 'I talked of preaching, and of the great success which those called Methodists have. Johnson: Sir, it is owing to their expressing themselves in a plain and familiar manner, which is the only way to do good to the common people. . . .'

Horace Walpole characteristically did not care for the enthusiasm when he heard Wesley in his later years: 'Wondrous clever, but as evidently an actor as Garrick. He spoke his sermon, but so fast, and with so little accent, that I am sure he has often uttered it, for it was like a lesson. There were parts and eloquence in it; but, towards the end, he exalted his voice, and acted very ugly enthusiasm.'

Methodism penetrated high society, and the Countess of Huntingdon, whose sister-in-law Lady Margaret Hastings had married Benjamin Ingham of the Holy Club, had much to do with this. Influenced by her sister-in-law, and also much affected by a serious

Selina, Countess of Huntingdon, one of the earliest and most influential of Wesley's followers, subsequently became a Calvinist, appointing as her chaplain George Whitefield. However, she remained a lifelong friend of the Wesleys.

illness, she was converted and to the dismay of her family 'turned Methodist'. Her husband asked his old tutor at Oxford to intervene, but Bishop Benson's attempts to influence her were unsuccessful. She was mainly responsible for introducing Methodism into aristocratic circles; her views even penetrated the court where Lord Dartmouth was converted. The religious meetings held in her drawing rooms were paralleled by similar meetings for the poor in her kitchens, and were a preliminary to a missionary campaign which she conducted throughout the country. She used her fortune and her prestige to provide chapels for the itinerant preachers who were her protégés.

It is generally believed that Lady Huntingdon was one of those who followed Wesley out of the Fetter Lane Society after his rift with the Moravians in 1739. In 1748 she appointed as one of her chaplains George Whitefield who, as we have seen, had by then moved away from Wesley into Calvinism. Whitefield influenced the Countess to do the same, but both remained on good personal terms with the Wesleys. In 1752, for instance, Lady Huntingdon nursed Mrs Charles

AN EASTERN VIEW of the Rev.ᵈ Mᵗ. Whitfield's NEW CHAPEL and ALMS-HOUSES in Tottenham-Court Road, MIDDLESEX, 1764

SCRIPTURE MOTIVES
To the ERECTION of a
NEW CHAPEL

EXOD. XX.
In all places where I
record my Name, I will
come unto thee; and I
will bless thee.
EXOD. XXX.
At the Door of the Taber-
nacle of the Congrega-
tion, I will meet thee, and
there I will Speak unto thee.
EXOD. XL.
When the Tabernacle was
set up, the Glory of the Lord
filled the Tabernacle.

SCRIPTURE MOTIVES
To the ERECTION of the
NEW ALMS-HOUSES.
I.TIM. VI.
Charge them that are rich,
to be ready to distribute.
GAL. VI.
As we have Opportunity,
let us do Good unto all Men,
especially to them who are
of the Houshold of Faith.
HEB. XIII.
To do good and communicate
forget not: for with Such Sacri-
fices God is well pleased.

Whitefield's Tabernacle in Tottenham Court Road became a centre for the Calvinist movement directed by the Countess of Huntingdon.

Wesley through smallpox, and in 1762 attended Wesley's Conference at Leeds. As for Whitefield, though he and Wesley remained doctrinally at odds with each other, their mutual respect and affection won through.

In 1770, the year of Whitefield's death in America, Wesley was himself contemplating another voyage across the Atlantic. 'I have some thoughts of going to America,' he wrote, 'but the way is not yet plain.' The following year he considered that 'I have no business there as long as they can do without me'. With the War of Independence only a few years away, Methodism was beginning to expand in America. The 1769 Methodist Conference had sent out two preachers, and in 1771 these were followed by Richard Wright and Francis Asbury. The first American Methodist Conference was held in 1774, when membership was less than 3,000. By 1784 the number had increased to 12,914, and in 1790 it stood at no less than 57,631, a rate of growth far exceeding that of any other Protestant organization in the world.

Asbury, the son of a Staffordshire tenant farmer and of an intensely religious Welshwoman with high ambitions for her child, played an essential part in this phenomenal expansion. He has been called 'the Wesley of America', and, like Wesley, possessed extraordinary dedication and physical endurance, and revealed great gifts of diplomacy and organization. By these talents he earned a special place in the history of the foundation of the Methodist Church in America. After the Southern Conference of 1779 he became virtually the head of the Methodist organization there.

Wesley's attitude towards American independence was initially sympathetic, in spite of his strong monarchist principles. Commenting in 1771 on the British government's measures against the colonists, he wrote, 'I doubt whether any man can defend them either on the foot of law, equity or prudence.' In 1775 he sent an impressively objective letter to the Prime Minister, Lord North, in which he wrote: 'I do not intend to enter upon the question whether the Americans are in the right or in the wrong. Here all my prejudices are against the Americans; for I am an High Churchman, the son of an High Churchman, bred up from my childhood in the highest notions of passive obedience and non-resistance. And yet, in spite of all my long-rooted prejudices, I cannot avoid thinking, if I think at all, these, an oppressed people, asked for nothing more than their legal rights, and that in the most modest and inoffensive manner that the nature of the thing would allow. . . .

'These men think, one and all, be it right or wrong, that they are contending *pro aris et focis*, for their wives, children, and liberty! What an advantage they have herein over many that fight only for pay, none of whom care a straw for the cause wherein they are engaged, most of whom strongly disapprove of it! Have they not another considerable advantage? Is there occasion to recruit the troops? Their supplies are at hand and all round about them: ours are three thousand miles off! . . .'

But the same year of 1775 saw his *Calm Address to our American Colonies*, a defence of England's right to tax the colonists without granting them any representation, which he had abridged (without acknowledgment) from a pamphlet by Johnson. Accused of inconsistency he wrote, in a preface to the second edition, 'I was of a different judgment on this head, till I read a Tract entitled *Taxation no Tyranny*. But as soon as I received more light myself, I judged it my duty to impart it to others.'

After the Declaration of Independence he issued, in 1777, an even less tolerant statement of his views, entitled *A Calm Address to the Inhabitants of England*, in which he maintained that the shortest way to peace would be a victory for the British forces in America, and

Francis Asbury, sometimes known as 'the Wesley of America'.

denounced the rebels: 'Whatever they do, they will not fight. I believe they cannot, for the hand of God is upon them. But they can rob and plunder and destroy, and turn a well-peopled and fruitful land into a wilderness. . . . No man there can say that his goods are his own. They are absolutely at the disposal of the mob, or the Congress.'

The ending of the war accelerated a crisis in the policy and structure of Methodism which led finally to the break with the Anglican Establishment. Wesley asked the Bishop of London if he would ordain a preacher who would be sent to America. The Bishop refused. So in September 1784 Dr T. Coke was 'ordained' by Wesley himself 'to the office of Superintendent of the Societies in America'. The following year he ordained seven more for services at home and abroad.

When Coke reached America he was to ordain Asbury. 'I can by no means agree,' wrote Wesley in his journal, 'to leave such a field for

Thomas Coke, one of Wesley's most trusted lieutenants, was ordained by him as 'Superintendent of the Societies in America', thus causing the final schism between Methodism and the Church of England.

gathering souls to Christ as we have in America. . . . Therefore I am determined, by the Grace of God, not to leave them, let the consequence be what it may.'

It had been decided in England that Coke was to share his post with Asbury, but the latter insisted that the joint appointment should be made, not directly by Wesley, but by the Baltimore Conference. Thus he was well placed to dominate his colleague and, though ordained as deacon and elder (like Coke) of the Methodist Episcopal Church in America, became widely known as Bishop Asbury.

Asbury then went on to secure a special place for his Church by drawing up and presenting, with Coke, an address of congratulation to General Washington on his appointment to the Presidency: 'We are conscious, from the signal proofs you have already given, that you are a friend of mankind; and under this established idea, place as full

In North America the expansion of Methodism was even more rapid than in Britain, with Coke's ordination of Asbury (*above*) an important step in the organization of the Societies. *Right*, the Old Methodist Church in John Street, New York.

Opposite, above, the first Methodist Conference at the City Road Chapel, 1779. John, Charles, and 446 of his preachers are depicted. *Below*, General Oglethorpe aged 88, still kept up his acquaintance with the Wesleys.

confidence in your wisdom and integrity for the preservation of those civil and religious liberties which have been transmitted to us by the providence of God and the glorious Revolution, as we believe ought to be imposed in man.'

In England, John Wesley still ruled the movement through the Conference. He had intended Charles to succeed him, but the elder brother outlived the younger, who died in 1788. It was the Conference which carried the movement on, after the final break with the established Church.

In old age there was some slight degree of relaxation for the Wesleys, especially for Charles, who settled in Marylebone and commuted to City Road in his carriage. His marriage was successful. He had two sons who became well-known musicians. Though Charles still went about his work with ardour, the family kept a lively salon, which the gallant General Oglethorpe sometimes attended. When Charles died, his widow and sons decided that he should be buried at St Marylebone and not in the Methodist burying ground by the City Road Chapel, since this was not consecrated by the Church of England. The sons

James Oglethorpe

"He went about doing good."

I. Miller, del.t   R. Hancock, Sculp.

Rev.d John Wesley A.M.

were in fact resolutely opposed to the Methodist way of life, and one of them became a Roman Catholic.

Wesley's last years saw the triumphant expansion of Methodism, with membership increasing from 52,334 in 1780 to 134,549 ten years later. Wesley himself had the satisfaction of finally being recognized by the Establishment, recording that he now had 'more invitations to preach in churches than I can accept of'. His strength remained astonishingly good, and while in his eighties he continued his preaching tours throughout the length and breadth of the country.

In 1790, when he was approaching his 87th year, he wrote: 'I am now an old man, decayed from head to foot. . . . However, blessed be God, I do not slack my labour. *I can preach and write still.*' In fact, his preaching tours were little less demanding than they had been fifty years before, though he did now travel by chaise rather than on horseback.

Old age finally brought Wesley acceptance and recognition: *opposite*, 'He went about doing good', an engraving of 1790; *above*, preaching at Bristol before the Mayor and other dignitaries.

The Cathedral of Methodism: Wesley's Chapel in City Road ('perfectly neat, but not fine') was opened on 1 November 1778.

A week before the end came, in 1791, he wrote what is believed to be his last letter – to the young abolitionist William Wilberforce: '... Go on, in the name of God and in the power of His might, till even American slavery, the vilest that ever saw the sun, shall vanish before it.' The next day he grew weaker, and it became clear that his life was beginning to slip away. His last hours were as serene and peaceful as one might have expected. Towards the end he said in a clear voice: 'The best of all is – God is with us.' And this message he repeated with special emphasis, so that it has become one of the rallying cries of Methodism. *'The best of all is – God is with us!'* He died on the morning of 2 March 1791.

The building of Wesley's Chapel, City Road, sometimes called the Cathedral of Methodism, began in April 1777, after Wesley himself had issued an appeal for funds. Though the land was leased for a period of fifty-seven years, the foundation stone bore the inscription: 'Probably this will be seen no more by any human eye; but will remain there till the earth, and the works thereof, are burnt up.' In 1940 the Blitz ensured that this part of the earth, at least, came near to being burnt up, and the building was barely saved. 'We watched the tongues of flame darting out,' wrote a member of the Society, 'licking the side of Wesley's House around the Prayer Room window, then spreading into the buildings verging onto the graveyard. "Is this a church?" asked one of the firemen. "Wesley's Chapel," was the reply. "Then we must save it." They worked heroically, helped by our men. Just then I went

Above, Wesley's Tree at Winchelsea, Sussex, scene of John Wesley's last sermon in the open air, 1790, preached when he was 87. *Left*, the old man, a legend in his time, finally breathes his last, 2 March 1791.

Wesley's House, City Road, London: John Wesley's base from 1779 till his death. Next door to the City Road Chapel, it is now a museum.

upstairs and I heard someone say, "The wind has changed and it is blowing away from us".'

Wesley's religious influence on his own times, and subsequently on his own country and the Christian world, was profound. Whether his social or political influence was comparably extensive is another matter. He was after all a High Church Tory, frequently asserting his loyalty to the King. Both he and Charles were well aware of their social position and their Oxford background, even though they might move and work virtually without money among the poor, the artisan and the lower middle classes. 'The greater the share people have in government,' he wrote, 'the less liberty, civil or religious, does a nation

Wesley's House: the Prayer Room where Wesley prayed night and morning. '. . . I sit down alone; only God is here. In His presence I open, I read His book; . . . and what I thus learn, I teach.'

enjoy.' He actively encouraged the bourgeois – 'Gain all you can by using in your business all the understanding which God has given. . . . It is a shame for a Christian not to improve upon whatever he takes in hand.' The early Methodists actually condoned child labour, being convinced that idleness was a greater evil. Their opposition to the ordinary pleasures and diversions of the times contributed considerably towards the breakdown of the industrial revolution.

Thus it may be claimed that Methodism was politically regressive, a stabilizing influence advising submission to the Crown, the Government and the employers. Halévy's dictum that it prevented revolution in Britain in the 1790s is certainly supported by such evidence. On the other hand, Methodism brought to working people not only spiritual dynamism but also education, self-confidence, and a potential for self-organization which played an important part in subsequent trade unionism and radical politics. Even so, there is something paradoxical in the fact that a religion of the heart, typified by Charles's famous and often moving (thought sentimental) hymns, should have become notorious in the last century for inhibiting spontaneity.

Wesley had given instructions in his will that his funeral should be conducted with a minimum of display – he even forbade the use of a hearse. But the day before the burial his open coffin was placed in the City Road Chapel, and 10,000 people filed past to pay their last respects. The funeral itself took place very early in the morning and with deliberately little notice, but it was attended by a great crowd. John Wesley's life had begun almost with the new century; its end marked the close of an epoch.

JOHN WESLEY, M.A.

BORN JUNE 17, 1703: DIED MARCH 2, 1791.

CHARLES WESLEY, M.A.

BORN DECEMBER 18, 1708: DIED MARCH 29, 1788.

"THE BEST OF ALL IS, GOD IS WITH US."

Medallion of John and Charles Wesley at Westminster Abbey, dated 1875. The words commemorate John Wesley's final message before he died.

SELECT BIBLIOGRAPHY

John Wesley's *Journal*, ed. by N. Curnock, 8 vols (London, 1909–16).
John Wesley's *Letters*, ed. by John Telford, 8 vols (London, 1931).

BOWEN, Marjorie *Wrestling Jacob* (Kingswood, Surrey, 1937).
EDWARDS, Maldwyn *Family Circle* (London, 1949).
GREEN, V. H. H. *The Young Mr Wesley* (London and New York, 1961).
LEE, Umphrey *The Lord's Horseman* (Nashville, N.Y., 1954; London, 1956).
LUNN, Arnold *John Wesley* (London, 1929).
SIMON, J. S. *John Wesley, the Master Builder* (London, 1927).
TELFORD, John *The Life of John Wesley* (London, 1924).
TYERMAN, L. *The Life and Times of the Rev. John Wesley*, 3 vols (London, 1870–71).
VULLIAMY, C. E. *John Wesley* (London, 1931).

CHRONOLOGY

1703 17 June: birth of John Wesley, fifteenth child of Samuel and Susanna (*née* Annesley) Wesley, at Epworth rectory, Lincolnshire.

1707 Birth of Charles Wesley.

1709 9 February: rescue from a fire at Epworth rectory. 'A brand plucked out of the burning.'

1714 Admitted at the Charterhouse School.

1720 24 June: elected scholar of Christ Church College, Oxford.

1725 Ordained deacon. Preaches first sermon at South Leigh, nr Witney, Oxon. The 'Varanese' affair.

1726 17 March: elected Fellow of Lincoln College, Oxford.

1727 Takes up the curacy of Wroote, Lincs., on behalf of his father.

1729 Return to Oxford (November). Takes over leadership of the Holy Club.

1735 Death of J.W.'s father, Samuel. 14 October: sails for the new American colony of Georgia.

1736 6 February: arrives in Savannah. Meets the Moravian pastor Augustus Spangenberg.

1737 The Sophy Hopkey affair. 22 December: sails for England.

1738 Spiritual crisis. Meets Peter Boehler, the Moravian pastor (February). Joins the Fetter Lane Religious Society. 24 May: conversion at a meeting in Aldersgate St. Preaches the new doctrine of salvation through faith, and is barred from many London churches. Visits the Moravian settlement at Herrnhut (August) with Benjamin Ingham.

1739 2 April, Bristol: J.W. preaches his first open-air sermon. First Methodist chapel is built (May) at Bristol Horse Fair, and Methodist Societies formed. 11 November: opening of the Foundery, London's first Methodist chapel. Death of J.W.'s brother, Samuel.

1740 Separates from the Moravians, leaving the Fetter Lane Society. Sets up a school for poor children at Kingswood, Bristol. Accepts the principle and practice of lay-preaching. Beginning of mob violence against the Methodists and their property.

1741 Tours South Wales. Beginning of J.W.'s itinerancy.

1742 Visits the north of England, preaching at Newcastle and elsewhere. 6 June: preaches at

Epworth from his father's tomb-stone. Rapid expansion of Methodism. 23 July: death of Susanna Wesley, J.W.'s mother.

1744 First Methodist Conference held at the Foundery (June), confirming a division of the country into Methodist 'circuits'.

1746 Founds a dispensary for the poor.

1747 First tour of Ireland. Publishes *Primitive Physic*.

1748 Falls ill at Newcastle (August) where he is tended by Grace Murray.

1749 Officiates at the wedding of Charles Wesley to Sarah Gwynne. Goes with Grace Murray on a field tour of Ireland, where a form of engagement (*De praesenti*) is celebrated at Dublin. The proposed marriage is violently opposed by Charles Wesley and some other Methodists. Grace Murray is persuaded to return to her former fiancé, John Bennet, whom she marries (3 October).

1751 Marriage to Mrs Vazeille (February). First tour of Scotland (April).

1755 Serious breach between J.W. and his wife.

1768 Opening of a Methodist chapel in New York. Foundation of Lady Huntingdon's College at Trevecca.

1771 Francis Asbury, later known as 'the Wesley of America', sails across the Atlantic on his first mission.

1773 Outbreak of the American Revolution.

1775 J.W. publishes *A Calm Address to our American Colonies*.

1778 2 November: opening of the City Road Chapel, London.

1781 Death of J.W.'s wife.

1783 Visits Holland.

1784 J.W.'s ordination of Coke and others, for work in America, leads to an official break with the Anglican Church.

1788 29 March: death of Charles Wesley.

1791 23 February: J.W.'s last sermon (at Leatherhead, Surrey). 2 March: death of John Wesley.

LIST OF ILLUSTRATIONS

Matthew Prior. Oil painting; attributed to Dahl. National Portrait Gallery, London.

Alexander Pope. Chalk drawing by W. Hoare. National Portrait Gallery, London.

31 Richard Colley Wesley, family and friend. Oil painting by William Hogarth. By permission of the Duke of Wellington. Photo by courtesy of the Courtauld Institute of Art.

33 'The Holy Club in Session'. Engraving by S. Bellin after Marshall Claxton. The Methodist Church Archives and History Committee. Photo Eileen Tweedy.

34 James Harvey. Print from a portrait by Williams. British Museum.

John Gambold. Engraving by J. Spilsbury after A.L. Brandt. British Museum.

35 Bocardo Prison, Oxford. Etching. By courtesy of Oxfordshire County Libraries. Photo John Peacock.

'Scholars at a lecture.' Engraving by William Hogarth, 1736/7. British Museum.

37 'Mrs Delany at work', by Lady Catherine Hanmer. Lady Llanover collection. From *Mrs Delany* by R. Brimley Johnson, 1925.

'Selina' Ann Granville. Crayon drawing by Mrs Delany. Lady Llanover collection. From *Mrs Delany* by R. Brimley Johnson, 1925.

38 Mrs Delany. Drawing by an unknown artist. F. Wellesley Collection. British Museum.

39 'John Wesley greeting George Whitefield'. Engraving by S. Bellin after E.G. Lewes. The Methodist Church Archives and History Committee. Photo Eileen Tweedy.

40 Fleet Prison, interior. Engraving from Moses Pitt's 'The Cry of the Oppressed . . .' 1691. Guildhall Library, London.

41 General J.E. Oglethorpe. Engraving after the mezzotint by T. Burford, c. 1743. From *J. Edward Oglethorpe* by Ettinger. British Library, London.

42 Tomo-Chi-Chi, Creek Indian chief. Print from *Collections of the Georgia Historical Society*, Vol VII, Part II, 1911. British Library, London.

43 Count Zinzendorf in Paris, 1720. Painting by Alexander Simon Belle. From *Zinzendorf, the Ecumenical Pioneer*, by A.J. Lewis, 1962.

Benjamin Ingham. Nineteenth-century print. By courtesy: Leeds City Libraries.

44 Passenger list of the *Simmonds*. By courtesy: The Moravian Church House, London. Photo Eileen Tweedy.

45 'The John Wesley Missionary Ship'. Sketch and engraving by George Baxter. Wesley's Chapel, City Road, London. Photo Eileen Tweedy.

47 Augustus Gottlieb Spangenberg. Engraving by W. Dickes after a drawing by A. Graff. By courtesy: The Moravian Church House, London. Photo Eileen Tweedy.

48 Map of Georgia coastline. From a drawing by William de Brahm. From *John Wesley's Journal*, Vol I (1909 edition).

Savannah in Wesley's day. From a print, c. 1737. From *John Wesley's Journal*, Vol I (1909 edition).

49 'Charles Wesley Preaching to the North American Indians'.

Nineteenth-century print. Wesley's Chapel, City Road, London. Photo Eileen Tweedy.

52 Facsimile page from John Wesley's Journal in Georgia. From *Wesley and his Century*, by the Rev. W.H. Fitchett, 1906.

55 Peter Boehler. Lithograph from a drawing by Krugestein. By courtesy: The Moravian Church House, London. Photo Eileen Tweedy.

56 Love-feast Cup. Wesley's Chapel, City Road, London. Photo Eileen Tweedy.

57 Map of Aldersgate. From *John Wesley's Journal*, Vol I (1909 edition).

59 Samuel Wesley (brother). From *Epworth . . . the home of the Wesleys* by W. Le Cato Edwards. Photo by courtesy: Rev. W. Le Cato Edwards.

James Hutton. Engraving by J.R. Smith after the oil portrait by R. Cosway. By courtesy: The Moravian Church House, London. Photo Eileen Tweedy.

Blundell's School letterhead, 1726. Design by William Hogarth. British Museum.

61 Herrnhut. Engraving, 1756. By courtesy: Archiv der Brüder-Unität, Herrnhut, D.D.R.

Count Zinzendorf with dignitaries. By an unknown artist. National Portrait Gallery, London.

62 'The Idle 'Prentice Executed at Tyburn'. Engraving by William Hogarth, 1747, Plate II of 'Industry and Idleness' series. Guildhall Library, City of London.

63 'Gin Lane'. Second state. Engraving by William Hogarth, 1750/1. British Museum.

64 George Whitefield. Oil painting by J. Woolaston. National Portrait Gallery, London.

65 'Credulity, Superstition and Fanaticism'. Engraving by William Hogarth, 1762. Guildhall Library, London.

'Enthusiasm delineated' (detail). Engraving by William Hogarth, *c.* 1761. British Museum.

66 View of Bristol (docks). Eighteenth-century painting. City of Bristol Museum and Art Gallery.

View of Bristol (glasshouses). Engraving by Heath after E. Bird, 1809. Avon County Library. Photo Eileen Tweedy.

67 Methodist Society Ticket. National Monuments Record. Photo C.F. Stell.

68 Richard (Beau) Nash. Engraving by A. Walker after Hoare. British Museum.

69 John Cennick. Engraving by R. Pucelle after Jenkins. By courtesy: The Moravian Church House, London. Photo Eileen Tweedy.

Thomas Maxfield. Engraving by Houston after T. Beach. British Museum.

70 Methodist preaching at Upper Moorfields. Engraving by Robert Pranker after John Griffiths, 1750. British Museum.

71 John Nelson. From *Wesley His Own Biographer*, London, 1891.

72 Bristol, The New Room (exterior). By courtesy: The New Room, Bristol. Photo Eileen Tweedy.

73 Bristol, The New Room (Wesley's Chapel). By courtesy: The New Room, Bristol. Photo Eileen Tweedy.

Bristol, The New Room (Wesley's Room). By courtesy: The New

Room, Bristol. Photo Eileen Tweedy.

74 The Foundery. An old print. Wesley's Chapel, City Road, London. Photo Eileen Tweedy.

75 Plan of Moorfields. Nineteenth-century print. Wesley's Chapel, City Road, London. Photo Eileen Tweedy.

76 'The origin of Sunday Schools'. Engraving by Leopold Lowenstam after Robert Dowling. Late eighteenth century. By permission of the County Archivist, Tyne and Wear County Council.

77 Kingswood School, Bristol. Drawing by T. M'Greary. By courtesy: The New Room, Bristol. Photo Eileen Tweedy.

78 Turnpike road near Oxford. Drawing (1777–81) by S.H. Grimm. Kaye Collection, British Museum. British Museum.

79 Dinner in Brockley Coomb (1788). Drawing by S.H. Grimm. Kaye Collection, British Museum. British Museum.

Letter from John Wesley to James Hervey, Oct 25, 1739. By courtesy: Lincoln College, Oxford. Thomas-Photos, Oxford.

80, The South-East Prospect of
81 Newcastle-upon-Tyne. Engraving from *View of Towns* (1745), Vol 2, by Buck. British Museum.

82 John Wesley preaching on his father's tombstone. Nineteenth-century print from a painting by George Washington Brownlow. Wesley's Chapel, City Road, London. Photo Eileen Tweedy.

83 Burial of Mrs Susanna Wesley. Engraving by Gunter after Wolstenholme. Guildhall Library, London.

Visit of John Wesley to his mother's grave 1779. Engraving by Hunt after Lee. Guildhall Library, London.

84 Susanna Wesley. Engraving by Owen after Williams. Wesley's Chapel, City Road, London. Photo Eileen Tweedy.

85 Riot at Wednesbury. From *Wesley His Own Biographer*, London, 1891.

87 Preaching at Nottingham. From *Wesley His Own Biographer*, London, 1891.

88 Ferry over the Trent. Lithograph by Charles John Smith. From *History and Topography of the Isle of Axholme*, by W.B. Stonehouse, 1839.

89 Map of Cornwall. Drawing by Bickham, 1750. County Museum, Truro. Photo Camera Craft, Truro.

90 John Wesley preaching near Gwennap, Cornwall. Nineteenth-century print. Wesley's Chapel, City Road, London. Photo Eileen Tweedy.

92 Apothecaries' Hall, 1830. Engraving by Hindihill after H. Shepherd. By courtesy: Worshipful Society of Apothecaries. Photo Eileen Tweedy.

John Wesley's electrification machine. Wesley's Chapel, City Road, London. Photo Eileen Tweedy.

Primitive Physic, text. By courtesy: Lincoln College, Oxford. Thomas-Photos, Oxford.

93 The Newcastle orphan house. From *Wesley His Own Biographer*, London, 1891.

94 South-East Prospect of Leeds. Engraving by Buck, 1745. By courtesy: Leeds City Libraries.

95 Sarah Gwynne. Oil painting by John Russell. By courtesy: The New Room, Bristol. Photo Eileen Tweedy.

Charles Wesley. Engraving. Artist unknown. British Museum.

Charles Wesley's house, Bristol. An old print. By courtesy: Charles Wesley's House, Bristol. Photo Eileen Tweedy.

98 Mrs Vazeille. Artist unknown. The Methodist Church Archives and History Committee. Photo Eileen Tweedy.

99 The Bank, Threadneedle Street. Aquatint, 1781, by T. Malton. Guildhall Library, London.

'Noon', from 'The Four Times of the Day'. Engraving by William Hogarth, 1738. British Museum.

100 Commemorative teapot. Wesley's Chapel, City Road, London. Photo Eileen Tweedy.

Wedgwood teapot. Wesley's Chapel, City Road, London. Photo Eileen Tweedy.

102 John Wesley portrait. Engraving by W. Ward after Romney(?). By courtesy: The New Room, Bristol. Photo Eileen Tweedy.

103 Relics of John Wesley's journeys. Wesley's Chapel, City Road, London. Photo Eileen Tweedy.

104 Heptonstall Chapel. Photo *The Times*.

105 Countess of Huntingdon. By an unknown artist. National Portrait Gallery, London.

106 Whitefield's Tabernacle. Print, London, 1764. Libraries and Arts Department, London Borough of Camden. Photo Eileen Tweedy.

108 Francis Asbury. Oil portrait by W. E. Whitehouse. The Methodist Church Archives and History Committee. Photo Eileen Tweedy.

109 Thomas Coke. Oil portrait by H. Edridge, 1799. National Portrait Gallery, London.

110 Ordination of Francis Asbury by T. Coke. By an unknown artist. The Methodist Church Archives and History Committee. Photo Eileen Tweedy.

Old Methodist Church, New York. An old print. Wesley's Chapel, City Road, London. Photo Eileen Tweedy.

111 The first Methodist Conference to be held in London, 1779. Contemporary print. The Methodist Church Archives and History Committee. Photo Eileen Tweedy.

General Oglethorpe, aged 88. Pen and ink sketch by S. Ireland, 1785.

From *Wesley His Own Biographer*, London, 1891.

112 John Wesley as an old man. Engraving by R. Hancock after I. Miller. British Museum.

113 John Wesley preaching before the Mayor and Corporation of Bristol. Oil painting by William H.O.Y. Titcomb. City of Bristol Museum and Art Gallery.

114 Wesley's Chapel, City Road. Engraving by Basire after Hindmarsh, 1779. Libraries and Arts Department, London Borough of Camden. Photo Eileen Tweedy.

115 Wesley's Tree, Winchelsea. Nineteenth-century print. Wesley's Chapel, City Road, London. Photo Eileen Tweedy.

Death of the Rev. John Wesley. Oil painting by Marshall Claxton R.A., 1842. By courtesy: The Methodist Church, Overseas Division (MMS.).

116 Wesley's house, London (exterior). Photo Eileen Tweedy.

117 Prayer Room, Wesley's House, London. Photo Eileen Tweedy.

118 Medallion, Westminster Abbey. Executed in marble by James Adams-Acton. Dated 1875. By courtesy: Dean and Chapter of Westminster.

INDEX

Figures in italic refer to illustration pages